privacynation

The Business of Managing Private Information and Documents

RANDOLPH A. KAHN, ESQ., DANIEL J. GOLDSTEIN, ESQ.,
AND BARCLAY T. BLAIR

Other Books from the Authors

From Randolph A. Kahn, ESQ.

Information Nation Warrior: Information Management Compliance Boot Camp

Information Nation: Seven Keys to Information Management Compliance

E-Mail Rules: A Business Guide to Managing Policies, Security, and Legal Issues for E-Mail and Digital Communication

From Barclay T. Blair

Information Nation Warrior: Information Management Compliance Boot Camp

Information Nation: Seven Keys to Information Management Compliance

Secure Electronic Commerce (Editor)

Professional XML (Editor)

About the Authors

Randolph A. Kahn, ESQ. is an internationally recognized authority on the legal, compliance, risk management, retention, and policy issues of information management. Mr. Kahn is the 2004 & 2005 recipient of the Britt Literary Award and is the founder of Kahn Consulting, Inc.

Daniel J. Goldstein, ESQ. is a privacy consultant in the San Francisco Bay Area and a member of the State Bar of California.

Barclay T. Blair is a consultant and internationally acclaimed speaker and author specializing in the compliance, policy, and management issues of information technology. He is Director of the IT Compliance Practice at Kahn Consulting, Inc.

privacynation

The Business of Managing Private Information and Documents

AIIM
Silver Spring, Maryland,
United States
Worcester, United Kingdom

RANDOLPH A. KAHN, ESQ., DANIEL J. GOLDSTEIN, ESQ., AND BARCLAY T. BLAIR

The authors have taken care in the researching and writing of this book. However we make no warranties of any kind and assume no responsibility for any mistakes, errors, misinterpretations, or omissions. Given the evolving legal and technical environments in which this book was drafted, the contents of the book may be time limited. In any event, before taking any action in response to any material contained in the book, please consult a professional to address your particular question or issue. The authors do not assume any responsibility or liability in any way arising out of or in connection with this book.

This publication is intended to provide authoritative and accurate information regarding its topic, but is sold with the understanding that neither the authors nor the publisher are engaged in providing legal advice or other professional service. Those requiring legal advice or the assistance of experts should consult a competent professional.

Library of Congress Cataloging-in-Publication Data

Kahn, Randolph.

Privacy nation: the business of managing private information and documents / by Randolph A. Kahn, Esq., Daniel J. Goldstein, Esq., Barclay T. Blair.—1st ed.

p. cm.

Includes bibliographical references.

ISBN 0-89258-411-4 (alk. paper)

1. Management information systems—United States. 2. Information technology—United States—Management. 3. Business records—Data processing—Management. 4. Business records—Law and legislation—United States. 5. Disclosure of information—Law and legislation—United States. I. Goldstein, Daniel J., 1962 II. Blair, Barclay T. III. Title.

HD30.213.K347 2006

658.4'038—dc22   2006000986

Design by Jane Firor & Associates, cover illustration by Vanessa Sifford, Production by OmniStudio, and Printing by Port City Press/Cadmus.

Special discounts on bulk quantities of AIIM publications are available upon request. For details, contact AIIM publications, 1100 Wayne Avenue, Suite 1100, Silver Spring, MD 20910, U.S., 301-587-2711. www.aiim.org

Dedications

Randolph A. Kahn, ESQ.
To my dearest family: Melissa, Dylan, Lily, and Teddy who make my life full, rich and joyous.

Daniel J. Goldstein, ESQ.
For Trista and Mia Devi.

Barclay T. Blair
To my family and friends.

Acknowledgements

The authors would like to acknowledge the support and encouragement of their friends, family, and clients who supported them and contributed to the creation of this book.

In addition, we would like to thank Patrick Strawbridge for his invaluable contribution and editorial review.

Table of Contents

Who Should Read This Book

Privacy is every organization's problem. Every employee in your organization plays an increasingly important role in managing private information. Managing privacy in today's business environment requires a concerted effort from all employees—whether it is the compliance department ensuring that employees are following required procedures, the information technology department providing adequate security, lawyers helping the organization interpret what is required, or a front-line employee taking information from a client or customer. Everyone must play their part in managing the information that is so valuable to your organization. The failure of a single employee to safeguard private information could leave you and your organization facing serious criminal or civil liability. Avoiding government investigations and costly lawsuits requires more than the effort of one individual; your whole organization must formulate and execute a plan.

Many books about privacy are designed to help consumers understand their privacy rights? Other privacy books are written for lawyers specializing in privacy law and its related issues.

While *Privacy Nation* contains information that may have value to consumers and lawyers, the primary focus of this book is on helping business people and managers understand the impact of privacy issues on their business.

Privacy Isn't My Problem, or Is It?

If your organization engages in any of the following kinds of activities, then *Privacy Nation* is for you:

- Does your organization collect non-public information about your customers? Do you notify them about what is being collected and how you manage it?

- Does your business mine data about customers' buying habits and/or product preferences?

- Does your organization share customer data across the company or with other business partners?

- Do employees transmit non-public personal information about customers or other individuals via email, fax, or instant messaging? Are there rules that regulate what gets shared and with whom?

- Do employees maintain non-public consumer data on computers with Internet access?

- Do employees maintain sensitive information on laptop computers or take laptops on business trips?

- Is information classified according to content at your organization? Do rules tell employees how to manage various classes of information?

- Does your organization have a privacy policy and are employees required to acknowledge that they understand it and what it requires? Do they understand the consequences if they fail to follow it?

- Does your company transfer unencrypted non-public consumer data to any third parties?

- Are company computers adequately protected from hackers in search of non-public consumer data or other confidential business information that you maintain?

- Do you have affiliate marketing programs with other commercial businesses?

- Do you collect dates of birth, credit card information, and/or email addresses on your website?

- Does your organization donate or sell computers it is no longer using?

- Do you operate a Wi-Fi network?

If you've answered yes to any of these questions, you will likely have a privacy problem on your hands in the near future if you don't already have one now.

Privacy Nation will help you—the business person or manager—understand how privacy impacts your organization today. *Privacy Nation* provides practical solutions that will help you understand how to manage the private information you collect in a manner that complies with the law, addresses your customer's demands, and protects your organization.

Preface

By John F. Mancini

The subtitle of this book—*The Business of Managing Private Information and Documents*—captures the intersection of three major trends that threaten to overwhelm many businesses and organizations. The trends the subtitle alludes to are:

1. The *explosion of business value* (and risk) centered on electronic information.

2. Increasing consumer concerns about *privacy and private information.*

3. Growing complexity related to *document security and integrity.*

Privacy Nation is all about the intersection of these three key trends. The companies and organizations that manage to navigate the challenging waters represented by these trends will be those that thrive and prosper. For those who do not, the future holds the distinct possibility of loss of consumer trust, erosion of sales and profits, and increased threat of litigation.

Trend #1: The explosion of business value (and risk) centered on electronic information. A recent survey by the Pew Internet Project captures the explosive change in customer and constituent expectations of companies, organizations, and governments. According to the Pew Internet Project, 93 million Americans age 18 and older have used the internet for health or medical purposes. 83 million have bought products online. 29 million Americans have researched or applied on-line for government benefits. There are over 60 million home broadband users. There are countless other examples pointing to exponentially increasing stakes in how electronic information is managed to meet and exceed customer and constituent needs. The "amazing" of customer expectations has created an environment in which *every* electronic interaction (phone, web, email, documents) is expected to approach the levels of service they receive from the *best* experience they ever received.

Trend #2: Increasing consumer concerns about privacy and private information. At the same time that consumers are raising the bar in terms of service expectations, they have an often conflicting concern about the information that must be maintained and managed to support these expectations. According to Forrester Research (July 2004), 61% of consumers say that they have privacy and security concerns that make them hesitant to give out credit card information online. In addition, one-half of respondents said they have concerns about creating a personalized portal on a Website. According to the Federal Trade Commission's Consumer Sentinel complaint database, identity theft is now the top complaint of consumers, accounting for nearly 40% of all complaints received. Identity theft and fraud complaints rose by 17 percent between 2003 and 2004 (from 542,378 in 2003 to 635,173 in 2004).

Trend #3: Growing complexity related to document security and integrity. According to Ken Rutsky from ZDNet, last year the Pentagon posted a report on its Website that contained classified information, including the name of a U.S. soldier who had accidentally shot and killed an Italian secret service agent in Iraq. The report was posted online in an unsecure PDF (Portable Document Format) document, enabling Web readers to access blacked-out, top-secret information on the PDF document through a simple cut and paste of the censored text. Gartner and IDC Research estimate that more than 1.8 trillion business documents and 2.4 trillion e-mails are created annually, and that 25 to 30 percent of all e-mails contain document attachments, which are riddled with business and technical risks that threaten privacy, compliance and security.

The Business of Managing Private Information and Documents is not easy. Developing an integrated strategy across the organization requires senior management commitment and an appreciation of complex and sometimes conflicting business, legal, privacy, and technology factors. This book is an important first step in helping organizations develop such a strategy.

John F. Mancini
President, AIIM

Introduction

As part of routine business, an employee sends an email containing the medical records of another employee to the company's insurance carrier. In a hurry, however, the employee misaddresses the email, which ultimately lands in the mailbox of a third party. Although the email contains a standard privacy notice advising unintended recipients to refrain from reading the message's contents, this warning appears at the end of the message. Thus, the third party does not receive the warning until she has already read the message. The damage is done. This minor mistake has major consequences—the company's privacy policy has been violated, and the affected employee may have legal claims arising under state and federal law—all because of a misaddressed email. Every day in business, employees accidentally misaddress email messages. With no clear policy to prevent it, no security precautions to protect the content, and no training telling employees how to handle the situation, this simple and common mistake snowballs into a major legal headache.

A sales person traveling across the country goes through security in Dallas, forgetting her laptop computer at the security check point. The computer is apparently taken by another traveler; along with it go files containing company secrets and confidential information. Making matters worse, the customer data on her computer included personal contact information from customers in California. The company's chief compliance officer in New York determines that the company needs to notify ALL of its customers in California (because of a new California law) unless they can precisely identify the information that was on her computer and the customers affected. The cost of disclosure pales in comparison to the bad press and lost customer confidence.

As these examples indicate, in today's business environment, managing information is more challenging than ever. There are three principal reasons for the increased need to manage information. First, there is more information than ever before. Second, that information is spread across organizations in a variety of forms. Finally, employees have the ability to access and transmit this information with the click of a button. With so much information stored in so many places and used by so many people, fiscal health and business accountability are directly tied to information management. Organizations that collect, store, and use private information are likely obligated to protect particular information from falling into the wrong hands. In other words, these organizations must ensure that private information remains private.

If you are in business of any kind (even the business of government), you likely collect, use, transmit, and maintain all sorts of personally identifiable information (PII) about customers, employees, clients, and business partners. These people expect that their information will remain confidential and secure. People like to do business with—and are more inclined to share information with—organizations they trust. Manage the privacy relationship with your customers and more business will flow from the relationship. Breach the trust just once and the relationship is forever changed.

When users of an Internet Service Provider (ISP) are deluged with a new spate of spam, or when online customers discover that their identity has been used to open bogus credit accounts, they will likely not care that their problems resulted from the actions of an untrustworthy employee. What they will care about is that the company did not protect their information. They likely expect their email address, like all personal information, will be properly secured from such events.

If your organization is not taking steps to ensure the privacy, integrity, and security of this data, you are a slow-moving target. When it becomes apparent that your organization failed to properly secure private information, you will find yourself in the crosshairs. Whether it's the Federal Trade Commission, the local office of the Better Business Bureau, state attorneys general, plaintiffs' lawyers, or consumer advocacy groups, when you fail to properly manage PII, a number of adversaries are prepared to make you and your organization pay for your mistakes.

The value of taking necessary steps to protect PII is confirmed by a quick spin through some recent representative news headlines. Don't you think the executives of these companies would have accepted the cost and effort of preventative planning to avoid this kind of news coverage?

- Online Retailer Agrees to Pay Up to $1.9 Million to Settle Privacy Lawsuit
- FTC Imposes $400,000 Payment to Settle COPPA Civil Penalty Charges
- Former Employee Pleads Guilty to Scheming to Steal Credit Reports in Massive ID Theft Case
- Pharmaceutical Giant Settles FTC Charges After Disclosing Email Addresses of 669 Users of Popular Anti-Depressant
- Organized Crime Rings and Petty Thieves Flocking to the Internet
- Security Flaw Allegedly Exposed Customers' Personal Information to Other Web Users
- Pentagon Clerk Arrested for Selling Soldiers' Credit Card Info

Privacy Nation is intended to serve as a practical guide for managers in business or government whose job responsibilities include handling private information. It is a book about Private Information Management (PIM)—the manner in which businesses, government, and other entities should collect, maintain, and use personal information.

part I

Laying the Foundation for Managing Private Information and Documents

Why Privacy Matters

1

In a business environment that relies more than ever on data, individuals' PII is a valuable commodity. Technology has enabled the gathering, compiling, and transfer of PII and confidential business information with a speed and ease that could not have been anticipated just a few years ago. Clearly, the Internet has accelerated the rate of information collection and exchange, a practice that has been commonplace in the offline world for decades. Millions of Web surfers, particularly those who conduct business over the Internet, leave a trail of data that can be readily collected, categorized, maintained, and sold by businesses and individuals online and off. These data trails contain a wealth of information about a buyer's commercial preferences, and, in some cases, even more sensitive information such as medical history, income sources and levels, and criminal history.

So, why does privacy matter to your organization?

1) Properly managing information that customers expect to remain private is good for business. People like to do business with businesses they trust.

2) Although consumers want to maintain control over their PII, they also want the convenience of doing business through new channels such as websites, email, instant messaging, and telephone. To maximize the value of each business channel, you need to satisfy your customers that those channels are secure.

3) Failing to manage personal information can and does have serious financial consequences: direct penalties, government-mandated privacy controls, loss of reputation, bad press, loss of customer confidence, and more.

4) The e-world has spawned a new breed of criminals who seek to steal personal data, attack your networks, and put your business at risk. These criminals need personal information so they can exploit the data for economic gain. If this

You Make the Call: Who Would You Want to Do Business With?

- A company that has the cheapest price, but informs you upfront it will sell your personal information and credit card data to help defray some of their overhead costs.
- A company that is slightly more expensive, but says it is committed to taking reasonable efforts to secure your personal and credit card information. Despite these assurances, the company, on average, experiences a security breach once a week.
- A company that has made a significant investment in state of the art security measures, has an internal information security program and a proven security track record, and is also price-competitive.
- A company that has built the Taj Mahal of security around their e-commerce portal, has never had a breach (though many try to hack in), and is about twice as expensive.

If you are like most of us, you probably feel most comfortable doing business with the third company described because you balance security and price. This hypothetical company is not the most secure, but it is secure enough to make you feel like your information is protected. You could do business with the fourth company described but that would cost you twice as much and it probably is not necessary. You get the point—if given the chance we would make these kinds of risk management-based decisions, measuring enough security with a reasonable price.

happens to your business, you may find yourself spending far too much time trying to defend your organization's business practices and security procedures. Defending past actions does not drive business forward—it takes employees' "eye off the ball." The more time you have to spend on figuring out what went wrong, the less time you have to focus on core business activities.

Managing Privacy Is an Important Responsibility

Business folks need to view privacy protection as an essential risk management activity. The cost of protecting PII is no different than an insurance premium, paid to avoid the much larger cost incurred if you fall victim to data theft, the misuse of information, or a security breach. That perspective is the driving force behind any effective PIM program. Smart businesses recognize that they cannot afford to ignore consumers' expectation of privacy.

Legal departments, who may have their own perspective on privacy, are essential partners in the battle to promote customer confidence and retention. Generally, corporate counsel is focused on ensuring that the company is in compliance with the alphabet-soup of laws that mandate the protection of private information: the Gramm-Leach-Bliley Act (GLBA), the CAN-SPAM Act, the Health Insurance Portability and Accountability Act (HIPAA), the Children's Online Privacy Protection Act (COPPA) and the EU Data Protection Directive. Your organization's lawyers, however, should also be tapped for guidance on all aspects of PIM, not just those designed to ensure compliance with minimum legal standards.

Understand the Impact of Privacy on Your Bottom Line

Many business executives view privacy as a cost center—an item on the debit side of the ledger that has little or no measurable return. That view, however, is outdated. The fact of the matter is that an effective PIM program yields benefits beyond the confines of risk management. Organizations that handle privacy in a legal and responsible manner see an immediate payoff in the form of increased transactions—an item that fits neatly on the asset side of the ledger.

Keeping Old Customers

Responsible management of customer information helps your organization retain its current customer base. Failing to manage customer information will make even the most loyal client question the relationship. In a recent survey, bank customers confirmed that it would take only one misstep for them to lose confidence in their bank's ability to handle their private financial information.[1] A higher degree of customer loyalty is a medium- to long-term benefit of responsible privacy practices and resulting consumer trust. In business, the best customers are existing customers. They are comfortable conducting transactions with your organization and tend to purchase more, and with greater frequency, than new customers. Existing customers do not require the up-front cost needed to acquire new customers.

What Do Your Customers Expect?

The website administrator wants to run an idea by you. She is contemplating acquiring a new technology that not only places a "cookie" on the computers of those who visit your website, but also downloads a small code that will automatically notify her department whenever the visitor goes to a competitor's website. While there is some business appeal to the technology, you are asked for your thoughts about how your customers would react to this feature if they knew about it. What do you decide to do?

- Agree to allow the technology.
- Allow the technology but notify customers via email that you plan to use the new technology.
- Allow the technology but notify customers via small print in the modified online privacy policy that you plan to use the new technology.
- Refuse to allow the technology because it seems underhanded; customers would likely find the conduct reprehensible.

If, while reading the above, you wondered where you can buy such technology (it already exists), you probably are heading down the wrong path. There are many things you can know about the customer base that would be useful and perceived as legitimate. This is not one of them. Taking control of someone's computer and having it automatically tell you when the customer is doing something on a competitor's website is probably going to anger most, if not all, of your customers. It may also violate existing business laws, along with the anti-spyware acts being contemplated in many jurisdictions.[2]

Attracting New Customers

A business with well-developed privacy practices will not only become more attractive to new customers, but will garner better, more accurate information about their customers. In fact, one of the downfalls of poor privacy practices is that consumers tend to provide false information to businesses they do not trust. A February 2004 survey of Internet users revealed that 70 percent of respondents had provided false data about their identity because of concerns about their personal information becoming public.[3] Whether this took the form of a fictional name, a fake telephone number, or false email address, the result for the business is the same: little usable information about a customer who is not confident about your service. There is a direct correlation between privacy, the quality of consumer data, and the success of continuing marketing efforts. When those who do not wish to receive communications have the chance to opt-out, businesses can stop throwing good money after bad prospects. Conversely, consumers who opt-in (indicate that they want to participate in some program or activity) are strong candidates for future transactions. When your business goes a step further and allows individuals access to PII maintained about them (one of the foundational elements of good privacy practices) it will reap the most accurate, up-to-date information you—and, more specifically, your marketing department—could desire.

The increasingly indisputable outcome of poor privacy practices is a negative impact to your bottom line. Perhaps the most immediate effect will be the loss of potential customers to competitors with better practices. The longer-term impacts include the high cost of defending alleged violations of privacy laws and the ensuing negative effects on your business.

How Did We Get Here? Distrust and Confusion Creating New Business Risks

Consider the following:

- An audiophile purchases a new home stereo system in the mid-1970s. He dutifully completes and mails the warranty card, and several weeks later begins to receive a catalog for automotive stereo equipment. The audiophile figures that the home stereo company has shared information about him with other related businesses. However, he is interested in automotive sound systems as well, and the convenience of receiving this targeted catalog outweighs his mild trepidation about his personal information and preferences being shared.

- Jump forward thirty years. A consumer makes an online purchase of diabetes supplies for her husband. Shortly thereafter, she begins receiving unsolicited email from pharmaceutical companies and medical supplies businesses. She begins receiving medical supply catalogs in the mail, and is frequently interrupted during dinner hours by telephone calls offering deep discounts on diabetic supplies. She, too, realizes that information about her and her husband has been shared, but she is outraged at the widespread distribution of what she considers highly personal information.

Consumers are more aware than ever that their detailed personal information is being gathered and used for a variety of purposes. Though information has been collected and shared for a long time by both the government and private companies, the benefits derived from having others know their PII apparently outweighed, in the past, any privacy concerns they had. Perhaps consumers felt that the information was unlikely to pass through the hands of more than a few companies. Most consumers had no expectation that their PII could be sold and spread across the globe for use by anyone willing to pay for access to it. Although the sharing of information doubtlessly resulted in some inconvenience, it was not of the level that led the public to demand new protection or laws.

Then came the Internet. Solicitations from people and businesses you've never seen or visited. The transmission of huge quantities of data at the click of a button.

Whatever patience the public had regarding the use, transmission, and sale of their PII in the old days has quickly been eroded with the Internet. As use of the Internet became widespread in the 1990s, especially as a tool for marketing and at-distance transactions, privacy concerns began to grow. And that awareness—combined with consumer confusion, distrust and a lack of clarity by businesses collecting and using PII—translated into increased risk for businesses that do not handle privacy in a responsible and legal manner.

Of course, the Internet provided the ideal mechanism for the collection and transfer of consumer data. PII could be gathered, with or without the individual's knowledge, and fired off to a third party with unprecedented speed and ease. And while many methods of information collection on the Internet are completely legitimate and ethical—such as the gathering of information necessary to make online purchases—businesses around the world often surreptitiously collect far more. This information might include the user's Internet Protocol, or IP address (a series of numbers which identifies individual computers), the type of Internet browser in use, as well as more revealing information such as what other websites he or she has visited while online. Some of this data, such as the IP address, may be necessary for the proper functioning of the website. However, other data serves non-technical purposes and can be combined with information volunteered by the website visitor (such as name, credit card number, delivery address, and so on) to create a detailed profile of the individual and his or her online activities.

Often, individuals' Web surfing habits and the sites they visit are ascertained through the use of technological tools such as cookies and spyware. The data gathered by these tools might also include more sensitive information such as the search terms they enter, purchases they make, and what banners they click-through. In the case of spyware, even individual keystrokes can be monitored, putting highly sensitive information at risk. Along with information volunteered through online shopping or website registration, the tool-gathered data can be used to build a detailed profile of a person based on his or her online activities. Naturally, these profiles are considered particularly valuable to legitimate businesses, but they are equally valuable to spammers, phishers, and other scammers online and off. It is these would-be thieves and fraudsters that make privacy a double-edged threat to business.

Anytime you collect information from a consumer, your business is taking a risk—even when you hire a third party to handle the data. Consider the case of a toy retail giant, which, in light of serious privacy allegations, settled a complaint with a state attorney general. The retailer's online division paid more than $50,000 in fines to stave off a lawsuit arising from its contractor's placing of cookies, without notification, on the computers of those who visited the toy seller's website.

Another of the major stumbling blocks with regard to PII is ownership. Certainly, consumers feel that they own their PII, and it would be hard to argue that someone other than an individual owns such common types of PII as a Social Security number, a driver's license number, or a credit card number. However, information—all information—is a commodity in today's business world. Therefore, it is common for businesses to claim ownership of precisely that information, particularly when they have paid considerable sums of money for it. The depth of PII available makes the issue that much more volatile. It would be nearly impossible for anybody doing business in the United States to avoid accommodating consumers' demand that they retain some element of control over such information.

Authenticating Customers: When Is Enough, Enough?

For companies doing any business with their customers online, whether it is making their account statements available, offering them products or services for sale, or any other business activity where personal information is exchanged, it is imperative that access to the system and information thereafter accessible on the organization's computers be sufficiently protected. In that regard, what was enough security two years ago may not be enough today. If IDs and passwords protected your online information treasure trove last year, perhaps your organization should now require two forms of authentication—passwords, IDs, and some other form of authentication protection like a smart card, security token, etc. In fact, in response to phishing and various other financial scams affecting banks worldwide, British banks are considering requiring two forms of authentication for customers.

What is a smart card and why does it matter?

A smart card is just a plastic card with various kinds of information on it or, more precisely, in it. Because it has a microchip embedded in it, a smart card can possess all sorts of information that can help protect PII and your identity. The smart card can be used to authenticate a person, so the smart card acts as another layer of identity protection.

And why shouldn't consumers be concerned? In one test by the Federal Trade Commission, an email address posted in a chat room began receiving spam within eight minutes of being posted.[4] Or take the ubiquitous grocery store loyalty cards. The data gathered on an individual's shopping habits is extensive and tells quite a bit about his or her life. Have they had a baby recently? Are they purchasing over-the-counter medicine? Do they eat certain types of food? These supermarket product choices will reveal information about one's family and lifestyle that is highly valuable to marketers of products that match the lifestyle. Or suppose an individual is accused of a crime. In a recent case, investigators examined purchasing information gathered from loyalty card transactions in an effort to tie an individual to an arson case. In another case, a drug retailer was forced to temporarily shut off its own Internet access to loyalty card information because the data was vulnerable to infiltration from outsiders.[5]

These are the kinds of issues that have led to today's high level of consumer distrust and confusion about commercial use and protection of their PII. For businesses operating in this environment, the most striking outcome has been the immediate need for better safeguarding of digital information, followed closely by the increased risk of consumer litigation or investigations by government agencies. The level of distrust of business, however, should come as no surprise, particularly in the aftermath of the Enron scandal and other corporate malfeasance of the late 1990s and early 2000s. In a national survey conducted in 2004, 66 percent of respondents agreed that, "if the opportunity arises, most businesses will take advantage of the public if they feel they are not likely to be found out."[6]

True or False: How are we doing at securing our corporate secrets, including PII?

The software developer of a popular instant messaging technology notified users that due to a security breach, users' computers and their contents can be accessed even in the absence of IM traffic, and even if the two parties never communicated.

Federal agencies are ordered to disconnect their websites from the Internet because inadequate security allows hackers to access original government records and alter, delete, and destroy them.

The website of a therapist dealing with some of the most heinous sex offenders inexplicably allowed anyone to view the offenders' medical records.

A drug company employee sent an email to users of one of their drugs and, in the process, revealed the PII of other users in violation of the law and the company's own privacy policy.

If you answered "true" to all of the above scenarios, you are correct. Unbelievable as it seems, major disasters regarding management of information have become commonplace.

Despite the best efforts of many businesses to manage PII responsibly and regain some lost consumer trust, the opportunity for misuse, loss, or theft of PII has continued to rapidly expand. High profile cases merely serve to reinforce consumer beliefs that it is difficult for businesses to completely eliminate risk of privacy breaches. The challenge is particularly daunting because the battle against security breaches must be waged against internal and external threats. A responsible organization must simultaneously defend its confidential information from two distinct classes of thieves: unscrupulous employees working from the inside and hackers who continually search for holes in security systems that seemed foolproof when installed. Staying a step ahead of those who would access PII illegally and/or for illegal purposes is a continuous challenge for business and the IT security industry.

Privacy Is Everybody's Problem

If you're conducting business anywhere in the world today, privacy is a problem that you have either come up against or will confront in the near future. It doesn't matter if you're a Fortune 500 company with a data warehouse full of consumer data or a mom-and-pop corner store with a small frequent buyer program. If you collect information about your customers or potential customers, privacy is your problem. In this environment, a business person ignores privacy concerns at his or her peril. Failure to address privacy in an effective manner has a variety of potential outcomes: loss of customers to businesses with better privacy practices, lawsuits, FTC investigations, and other negative consequences.

Lawsuits can be debilitating on a number of levels. The attorney's fees alone for defending a privacy-related case can easily reach several hundred thousand dollars, not including the cost of the inconvenience, the potential for a bad result, and the negative PR implications.

FTC investigations and ensuing actions should raise an equally loud alarm for the business professional. Unlike most private lawsuits, FTC privacy settlements may include mandated third party reporting to the FTC on businesses' privacy practices and compliance. These reporting requirements often run for many years and can include expensive, time-consuming, business-disrupting audits. The following chart includes just a few cases where the FTC imposed painful reporting obligations on companies for their failures.

Case	FTC Settlement: Reporting Requirement	Term
In the Matter of MTS, Inc., doing business as Tower Records/Books/ Video, a corporation, and Tower Direct, LLC, doing business as TowerRecords.com, a corporation. FTC File No. 032-3209[7]	Must have "a qualified third-party security professional" audit "its Website security" every two years.	10 years
In the Matter of Guess?, Inc., and Guess.com, Inc. FTC File No. 022 3260[8]	"Guess must have its security program certified as meeting or exceeding the standards in the consent order by an independent professional within a year, and every other year thereafter."	20 Years
In the Matter of Eli Lilly and Company. FTC File No. 012 3214[9]	Must conduct an annual written review of its information security program by qualified persons.	20 Years
In the Matter of Microsoft Corporation. FTC File No. 012 3240[10]	Must have its security program certified as meeting or exceeding the standards in the consent order by an independent professional every two years.	20 years

If you deal with privacy and digital information in a manner that gives due consideration to consumer demands and business needs, you will gain customers and long-term relationships. But when it comes to lawsuits and FTC actions, the only upside is avoiding them, and that is an upside well worth the investment.

Still having a hard time viewing privacy as your problem? After all, you're not a medical provider or a bank. These are the organizations that really need to be careful about privacy, right?

Wrong. Consider the types of privacy problems that have transpired for businesses beyond the usual suspects.

- A record store discloses customer data.

- A technology company has data of thousands of employees exposed when laptop computers are stolen from another firm they do business with.

- A computer security flaw exposes PII from customers of a wholesale supermarket chain.

- Forty million identities are stolen from a credit card company.

- A federal agency's lax security exposes PII.

- Media company employee information is exposed when tapes housing the information go missing.

Even the Federal Government's Management of PII is Subject to Scrutiny

In a June 22, 2005 *Wall Street Journal* article, the Transportation Safety Administration's storing of passenger data was called into question. Although the TSA publicly stated that it would not use information collected from passengers, "[t]he Transportation Security Administration acknowledged that it holds personal information from commercial databases on about 20,000 Americans..." When confronted by privacy advocates about the seemingly contradictory statements, the TSA reiterated, "the agency had 'adhered to the letter' of its past statement 'exactly'—partly because it was not looking at the data in question." Though having information is clearly different than using it, mere possession of PII creates management obligations.

In another glaring example that no organization is immune from privacy problems, the FDIC in June 2005 notified 6,000 employees that their information had been compromised. Dozens of cases of identity theft have been linked to this breach.

In fact, the U.S. House of Representatives Government Reform Committee issued a 2004 report card for the cybersecurity of federal agencies. Their overall grade: D+. A number of individual agencies were given Fs, including several departments that handle a trove of personal information: Health and Human Services, Homeland Security, Housing and Urban Development, and Veterans Affairs. In response to this performance, the committee instituted an informal network of IT security officers, so that successful departments could share their methods and plans for keeping private information private.[11]

Similarly, reviews by the Government Accountability Office (GAO) have found serious flaws in the information security operation of the Internal Revenue Service and Department of Homeland Security. Data at risk for unauthorized disclosure included "sensitive taxpayer information," and the GAO faulted Homeland Security for failing to take steps necessary to comply with federal law.[12]

If the federal government has trouble complying with its own laws, how confident are you in your data security?

Building the Foundation— Defining Privacy in the Digital Age

2

In an 1890 *Harvard Law Review* article, Samuel Warren and future United States Supreme Court Justice Louis Brandeis first defined the right to privacy as "the right to be let alone."[13] This definition seems quaint in the modern business era, where digital information propagates seemingly uncontrollably, and where an individual's personal information can be distributed to the far reaches of our world in a matter of seconds. Wherever that data travels, the people, businesses, or government agencies on the receiving end gain valuable insight into the subject individuals. What they do with that information ranges from the legitimate—transacting business, remitting credit card payments, and marketing activities—to the downright illegal and nefarious—sending spam, phishing, identity theft, and other fraudulent schemes. Increasingly, our lives as employee, employer, customer, client, and citizen are routinely interrupted. These interruptions impinge upon our "right to be let alone," even if just momentarily. Some would argue that the right to be let alone has evaporated in a blizzard of email, cell phone calls, and instant messaging.

The individuals who drafted the U.S. Constitution did not include any explicit provision that set forth a right to privacy. The Supreme Court has, however, ruled that there is a limited constitutional right of privacy based on several provisions in the Bill of Rights. This arises in part from the First Amendment's right of association; the Third Amendment's prohibition against quartering soldiers in a home; the Fourth Amendment's right to be secure in one's person, house, papers, and effects; and the Ninth Amendment's provision providing that unenumerated rights are retained by the people.[14] This concept of privacy, cobbled together from pieces of the Constitution, is not easily applied to the concept of privacy in the digital age, and, like the Brandeis/Warren definition, it does little to alleviate the growing concerns of business and consumers.

More than 100 years after the publication of the Brandeis and Warren article, and more than 40 years after the Supreme Court's seminal decision articulating the constitutional right to privacy, a modern business and legal definition of privacy is: **the right** to assert control over the collection, maintenance, transfer, security, and destruction by private and public sector organizations of an individual's personally identifiable information. PII consists of any information that can be used to identify a person, such as a name, postal address, Social Security number, driver's license number, email address, credit card number, or bank account number.

Modern Concepts of Privacy— at Home and Abroad

The federal government has begun to implement standards for the handling of private information. These concepts govern federal agencies' use of information in identifiable form (IIF). IIF includes information that is labeled by name or other personal identifiers (such as SSN or an account number), or information that can be linked to a particular person in other ways.[15]

The federal office that oversees government use of IIF has developed essential principles for agency handling of such material. Emerging principles include:

- **Accountability**—Assigned roles and responsibilities to assure that IIF is appropriately handled.

- **Notice**—Explaining to private individuals the agency's authority for collecting IIF; the purpose of the collection; the location of the entity maintaining the IIF; with whom the IIF may be shared and why; the rights an individual has in IIF; and the entity's polices, procedures, standards, and practices with regard to IIF.

- **Minimum Necessary**—Collection of IIF should be limited to only that information which the agency is authorized to collect and is minimally necessary for the agency's task.

- **Consent**—Before any IIF may be collected, the agency must obtain permission from the private individual.

- **Authorization**—An entity does not collect, use, or disclose IIF in a manner inconsistent with its Notice unless it has first obtained the individual's written permission for the use or disclosure.

- **Individual Rights/Individual Participation**—An individual should be afforded the ability to access and copy the IIF an entity acquired or maintains; obtain an accounting of disclosures that the entity made; request an amendment of the information an entity maintains and, if such amendment is not undertaken, request that the information be notated; and receive a confidential communication of IIF collection.

- **Limited Use/Acceptable Use**—Use and disclosure of IIF should be limited to the legal purpose set forth in an entity's Notice and then only to that which is minimally necessary to complete the legally permitted task. All other uses should be prohibited.

- **Data Accuracy/Data Integrity**—When possible, an entity relies first on the IIF it collects directly from the individual and it monitors access and modifications to that data.

- **Security Safeguards**—An entity implements the appropriate management, operational, and technical controls to preserve the privacy, confidentiality, integrity, and availability of IIF.

Privacy regulation in the United States is comprised of a mix of state law, federal law, industry-specific laws, and self-regulation. The laws and regulations that have emerged vary significantly from jurisdiction to jurisdiction and from industry to industry. This has resulted in a patchwork of privacy rules with a dizzying array of exceptions and loopholes.

The U.S. model sits in stark contrast to international privacy regulations such as the European Union's Data Protection Directive and Canada's Personal Information Protection and Electronic Documents Act (PIPEDA), both of which are comprehensive privacy laws

The Privacy Conflict Across the Pond

Test your understanding of the differences between U.S. and European-style privacy laws and regulations.

True or False?

1. Both American laws and European privacy laws are generally "technologically neutral," meaning they don't mandate the use of particular technology to secure PII.

False. The American legal system approach is technologically neutral. Under our laws, it generally does not matter how you arrive at a particular result, as long as you get there. This is not the EU approach. European laws make judgments about the particular technology used, and in some cases they mandate certain systems.

2. The EU is generally comfortable with the way American industry protects PII.

False. The Europeans have clashed with the United States government over several issues of PII management and protection. Indeed, the EU has concluded that American laws are insufficient to protect EU citizens' personal information. Europe also is dissatisfied with some of the restrictions regarding travel to and from this country. For example, the EU is only grudgingly agreeing to allow the U.S. government to store pictures of its citizens coming into the United States. The EU also has voiced displeasure with the United States terrorist database system.

3. EU and U.S. laws leave it to business to decide how best to manage data, including PII.

False. The EU is more proactive on laws restricting PII use. In fact, in the wake of terrorist bombings in Madrid in 2004 and in London in 2005, the EU has considered imposing requirements on ISPs to retain records of online traffic for up to three years. U.S. laws rarely require the retention or deletion of such information. An exception, however, is a new Federal Trade Commission rule requiring the proper destruction of certain credit report information.

that seek to provide clear rules with regard to the collection and use of PII.[16] Whereas the United States allows a person or organization to use PII unless it is forbidden by current law, in EU member states and many other nations, a person or organization may only use data if it is specifically permitted by law.

An example of the differences between American-style and European-style privacy schemes may be found in a recent Canadian ruling regarding business email addresses. Americans may doubt that one's work email address is "private" information; after all, the use of such email is generally restricted and it is freely disseminated on business cards, websites, and company directories. In Canada, however, the privacy commissioner's office ruled that business email addresses may be used only for the purposes for which they are distributed. Therefore, a solicitation to buy football tickets sent to a law professor's email address violated Canada's federal privacy law.[17]

Interplay Between the U.S. and European Systems

Because of the differences between the U.S. and European models of privacy regulation, special problems arise when data is transmitted through more than one country. Lawmakers in all nations have come to recognize that, in the Internet age, it is difficult to restrict all international exchanges of data. Nonetheless, governments are taking steps to protect PII in a global environment. The European Commission's Directive on Data Protection, for example, generally prohibits the transfer of the personal data of EU citizens to non-EU nations that do not meet the European "adequacy" standard for privacy protection.

For multinational organizations, global data exchange presents additional challenges to implementing an effective PIM program. Domestic and international laws are frequently inconsistent, and at times they may blatantly conflict. If your organization does business in more than one country, compliance with applicable privacy and data protection laws may require professional legal assistance. It is crucial that organizations doing business globally determine the applicability of all laws and address the requirements of each individual regulation. Take into account the risks that the laws seek to minimize, so that your compliance program addresses the riskiest areas first.

Governments Are Taking Privacy Seriously. So Should You.

Here's a list of just some of the privacy offices that have been set up worldwide:

Office of the Privacy Commissioner of Canada
Italian Data Protection Commission
Data Protection Commissioner of Ireland
New Zealand Privacy Commissioner
Office of the Hong Kong Privacy Commissioner for Personal Data
Polish Inspector General for the Protection of Personal Data
Swiss Federal Data Protection Commissioner
United Kingdom Information Commissioner
United States of America Federal Trade Commission
Cyprus, Office of the Commissioner for Personal Data Protection

Can I Contract My PII Obligations Away?

If you are obligated to protect PII, hiring a third party will not necessarily relieve you of your legal obligations. Like it or not, U.S. laws will likely apply to U.S. companies who outsource their data processing and data management, even if the work is performed by offshore companies.[18]

Managing Privacy Is Managing Risk

3

Businesses and consumers alike are well justified in their concern over the security of digital information, given the threat posed by criminals, identity thieves, and hackers. With or without new laws, the threat is likely to continue for the foreseeable future. In the short history of digital data and online networks, we have learned that data security cannot be absolute. Hackers continue to bypass security systems like modern-day safecrackers. In the past, stronger safes never really assured the security of the information maintained within if the safecracker was sufficiently skilled. Similarly, data security is a matter of risk reduction, not risk-proofing. You must put in place the safeguards that are adequate to reasonably protect the information that you maintain. The protections you choose will depend on a variety of factors, including the nature of the data, your industry, the size of your organization, and how much data it maintains.

From a risk management perspective, the amount of protection taken should correlate (more or less) to the sensitivity of the data. Such a "standard"—if something so vague can be considered a "standard"—is called for in several U.S. laws, although the precise level of security is rarely defined. When considering the security of your digital data, keep in mind that the risk you are trying to manage arises from several sources—theft or misuse, accidental exposure of PII, and lawsuits or other consumer actions based on noncompliance with governmental or industry standards.

The easy availability of and access to PII carries with it an inherent obligation of responsibility that businesses cannot afford to ignore. In some instances, this has risen to the level of individual safety. In 2004, an Internet information provider agreed to pay $85,000 to the estate of a New Hampshire woman murdered by a stalker five years before. In that case, an online investigative firm had sold the individual's Social Security number, work address, and home address to a second individual who used the information to locate the victim at her workplace. He then shot and killed her before taking his own life. In a preliminary ruling, the court held that the online information provider had a duty to exercise reasonable care in disclosing a third party's personal information to a client. Applied to other types of business, the ruling could have far-reaching impact on the standards of care that must be met when disclosing PII. Just think of how many businesses keep track of basic information like customer or employee names and addresses.

The point here is not to scare you with the specter of liability for somebody's death. Rather, we want to emphasize that the overwhelming predominance of consumer distrust spells potential trouble for business. The errors made in the cases above should give every business executive reason to pause and recognize the risk to his or her organization from both risk management and bottom-line perspectives.

In this regard, a primary objective of your data management practices must be to communicate to the public exactly what steps are taken to maintain the PII you collect in a secure manner. Such explanations ensure that individuals are informed of your maintenance and security procedures *prior* to their sharing of their information. If you operate in an online environment, your risk management initiatives should allow website visitors to view a policy describing these practices at every data collection point. The link to this policy should be prominent and easy to understand.

- Loss of customer confidence
- Resulting loss of business
- New laws
- Heightened scrutiny from regulators
- Imposition of mandatory practices
- Less electronic customer interaction and feedback

The less confidence a consumer has in shopping online, the less shopping that consumer will do. The *Wall Street Journal* reported that a 2005 Gartner survey revealed that "more than 42% of online shoppers and 28% of people who bank online are cutting back on their activity because of 'phishing' attacks and other assaults on sensitive data."

Question the Security of Your Networks and Confidential Business Information

Risks Created by Email Use

It is all but inevitable today that much of an organization's proprietary information, including consumer PII (along with financial data and legal information) will be transmitted via email. These messages may be transmitted down the hall or to the other side of the world, but regardless of physical distance, there are inherent risks to using this form of communication. Threats to the security and confidentiality of information contained in electronic communications and/or attachments arise at all stages during transmission and storage of the message.

Consider just a few of the risks associated with email use today, all of which pose a threat to your organization and its information assets:

- Mistakenly addressed or improperly delivered email containing unencrypted PII or other confidential information

- Being overrun with spam

- Losing legitimate messages because of spam-filtering technologies

- The interception of information by third parties using "packet-sniffing" technology

- Propagation of viruses, Trojan horses, or other malicious code on company computers or the network

- Failing to reliably authenticate the sender of an incoming email, and therefore risking the exposure of PII by replying to the message

- Losing control of company information on mobile email devices (and other hand-held and mobile computers)

- Exposing the company by attaching a laptop that has received infected email to the network

- Storing and retrieving email messages and attachments from a webmail service, which creates security issues involving the content and identity of recipients

There are technical solutions to all of these issues, but they are not used widely enough. For example, there are many secure email vendors in the market place. Simple encryption technology can help safeguard message content. Digital signature

Has Your Customer's Information Been Stolen?

Which of the following are clues that a customer's information has been taken and an ID theft may be in progress?

- Request for account contact information
- A change of the customer's address
- Fluctuations in spending patterns
- Atypically large purchases
- Purchases done in locations other than the home town of the customer

If you answered "all of the above," you would be correct. Though each of these activities may be legitimate, they are also leading indicators that the customer has been scammed or is the target of ID theft.

technology can be used to authenticate the identity of the sender of a message and to ensure that the content of the email was not altered after being sent. Technology may also provide a digital time stamp to confirm the date and time of transmission.

No matter which technology you choose to secure emails, there should be policies in place addressing permissible and impermissible uses of email in the workplace. These should include rules for the sending of PII and confidential business information via email. These rules will likely need to be drafted to provide specific guidelines for specific departments and job functions, depending on the nature of the business tasks involved. It is important that all employees understand who is—and who is not—authorized to use email to send PII, under what circumstances such information may be sent, and what security precautions must be followed. As always, the consequences for violations should be clearly communicated and enforced.

Monitoring Employees' Email: To Tell or Not To Tell

Sixty percent of companies surveyed by the American Management Association (AMA) reported they use software to monitor employees' incoming and outgoing email communications—a 13% increase from 2001. Of companies that use software, 13% also hired employees to physically monitor email.

From the perspective of a company trying to protect its business and legal interests, this only makes sense. Most companies that use email to do business consider their email systems company property, to be used only for company business. When an organization tells its employees the email is for business use only, employees shouldn't care that their email is being monitored, right?

Possibly. But in addition to informing employees that company email is company property, employers should also specifically inform employees that their email conversations may be monitored. This provides clear notice to employees that they have no expectation of email privacy in the workplace. When employees know "Big Brother" may be watching, they'll be less inclined to use the corporate email system inappropriately. This reduces litigation risks, the influx of spam, and potential security threats. However, it is important to remember that monitoring employee use of the company email systems may be prohibited in other countries even if you give them notice.

Instant Messaging: Let Your Policy Decide, Not Your Employees

In 2004 the Federal Deposit Insurance Company issued an unprecedented warning on the risks associated with the use of Internet instant messaging (IM) to banks and other financial institutions. As most business people—or anyone with a teenage son or daughter—know, IM enables nearly instantaneous online chat, as well as the ability to transfer files. However, widely available IM software may lack essential security features needed for secure use in business. Employees need to understand that public IM networks generally transmit unencrypted information; therefore, they should probably not be used to exchange PII or other sensitive business information. Data sent by IM is transmitted over the Internet and can be easily intercepted. And there is no reliable way, at least with off-the-shelf IM products, to authenticate the person on the other end of the communication. In other words, there is no way to verify that a message really originated from the sender with whom the recipient believes he or she is communicating during the session. Thus, the risk of being duped into sharing files or information increases with IM. Finally, public IM is vulnerable to worms, viruses, and other online threats associated with email. Because of these risks, IM raises a lot of red flags with respect to security, privacy, and potential legal liability.

If your organization wanted to block IM traffic altogether, it could. Firewalls can be configured to block incoming and outgoing IM traffic. Of course, this eliminates *all* IM traffic and prohibits its use as a business tool. For businesses that want to utilize IM's considerable advantages, technology vendors have developed IM products for corporate use that authenticate, encrypt, audit, log, retain, and monitor IM communication. Because IM has legitimate business benefits, it should not be ruled out as a safe technology.

Before deploying it at your organization, however, be sure you have addressed the risks and policy issues. Remember: technology before policy spells trouble.

Computer Search Tools

In response to the abundance of information now stored on PCs, a variety of search tools have been developed. These tools offer a quick way to search for information which may be hidden deep on the hard drive or is otherwise difficult to access. These tools can retrieve all types of electronic files, including webpages, and can even provide transcripts of IM conversations. For an educated user, search tools provide users nearly instant access to just about anything recently done on a computer. As worthwhile as these tools are, particularly with regard to employee productivity, there are a number of privacy concerns that arise from their potential misuse. Take, for example, an employee who maintains PII, including customers' credit card numbers and addresses, on her computer. If she walks away from her desk for just a few minutes, an unauthorized user can quickly and easily use the search tool to uncover the sensitive information stored on the computer, save it to a disk or attach it to an email, and gain permanent possession. Obviously, these search tools are too useful to be discarded. A prudent manager, however, will implement security precautions, such as requiring user authentication or password protection before a user may gain access to the tool.

Is That New Copier a Privacy Risk?

The digitization of the workplace has created privacy and data security concerns—even for some familiar, seemingly innocuous technologies. For example, digital photocopiers now contain hard drives that store information long after it is copied. Those same copiers may also possess the ability to receive and transmit data over the company's network—and across borders. Given these new capabilities, there may be features that need to be deactivated or controls that should be put in place in order to deal with the privacy issues. Digital copiers and fax machines receive and store volumes of customer and client PII, employee information, and other confidential business data each business day. This material once again is susceptible to being stolen by unscrupulous employees or hackers who have infiltrated your office network. Digital photocopiers must be subject to the same security considerations and solutions as other computers on and off your network. These might include data encryption software, firewalls, and other safeguards deemed appropriate by your IT team.

Is Your Wireless Network Secure?

According to a GAO report, many federal agencies do not have secure Wi-Fi networks. In fact, an audit of select agencies revealed that a passerby could glom onto government information with little effort.

If you operate a wireless network in your workplace, strong security precautions are required. Maintaining an unsecured wireless network is akin to making access to your network available to nearly any passerby with a computer. One very real risk is that without actually gaining access to your network, an unauthorized individual (albeit, a technologically skilled one) can capture, read, and save confidential digital data while it is in transit on the network. A recent study determined that 66 percent of U.S. banks are mistakenly broadcasting confidential information outside their walls via Wi-Fi.[21]

Once hijacked from your wireless network, private information can be used for a variety of illegitimate and illegal purposes. These uses might include identity theft, but there are other harmful uses. An interloper could simply alter the data and reintroduce it into the network, causing a potentially expensive and time consuming interruption of business.

Wireless networks also create the risk that people outside your company will attempt to use your wireless network for free

As the Worm Slithers

In 2004, the Cabir worm (another type of malicious code) was launched to attack wireless cellular telephones. The worm could grab your contacts list or engage in a whole host of other damaging activities. The potential assault on private information from viruses or worms is real. Today, no matter where PII is stored, it is potentially at risk unless properly protected. Just about every employee today has a cell phone with business contacts parked on them. What is your organization's liability if that information is disclosed?

Internet access. While this may seem an annoyance rather than a serious risk, virus writers, spammers, phishers, and other criminals could use the network to send out emails or other files anonymously. At the very least, the IT department and system administrators should install an intrusion detection system on any wireless network and should monitor it regularly. They must also keep up-to-date on new wireless network security threats and perform frequent risk analyses. Additionally, policies should be implemented that set out details regarding proper wireless devices and usage. Authorized users should be instructed not to transfer unencrypted PII or other confidential data over such a network.

Threats to Consumers Are Threats to Your Business

To secure the information your organization collects and stores, you need to do more than just make sure your own networks are protected. You also need to view the potential problems from the customers' end. Many of the threats to consumers arise outside your own business. By understanding what dangers lurk for those who provide information to your organization, you can better protect those users against data loss.

Identify All Potential Sources of Privacy Problems

Can you list some of the privacy issues that arise when the following technologies are used?

- Instant Messaging
- Interactive advertisements
- Blogs & Wikis (A Wiki is a blog in which any user can edit, add to, and delete previously provided content.)
- Newsgroups
- Wireless email
- Cell phones
- Electronic medical records
- PDAs

Identity Theft

Consumer alarm at the collection and transfer of PII has been driven not only by marketing intrusions such as increased spam, but also by the burgeoning problem of identity theft. Cases of identity theft have skyrocketed with the rapid adoption of online transactions and the resulting transfer of digital data. The FTC defines identity theft as a fraud that is committed or attempted using a person's identifying information without authority.[22] Identity theft occurs when a perpetrator obtains an individual's PII, such as credit card number or Social Security number, and uses this information to make purchases and/or open new accounts. In a recent period the FTC received more than half a million (516,740) reports of consumer fraud and identity theft.[23] During that time, consumers reported fraud-related losses in excess of $400 million. *And the cost to business was more than ten times that.*

These laws, however, have done little to allay the concerns of consumers or business, and identity theft remains a major driving factor in consumer privacy concerns. In fact, the Government Accountability Office took a look at the susceptibility of Social Security Numbers to unauthorized access and found that federal, state, and local governments could take steps to reduce the unnecessary exposure of SSNs in public records. The GAO report found that SSNs are exposed in a wide variety of public records, mostly at the state and local level. Although public access to such records is generally limited, the GAO estimated that 15 to 28 percent of the nation's counties put SSNs on the Internet, creating security risks for millions of individuals.[25]

Can I Be Sued for Allowing an ID Thief to Open an Account?

Despite widespread consumer frustration over the loss of control over their personal information, the courts have, so far, declined to recognize a specific duty on behalf of financial institutions to prevent fraudulent accounts from being opened.[26] However, because of increasing legislative interest and the unpredictability of future court decisions, any organization extending credit to new customers should be sure to verify the identities of those with whom they are doing business.

Enforcement and Organizational Vigilance is Needed to Reduce ID Thefts

State and federal enforcement of ID theft has picked up in recent years. But proactive enforcement is difficult, if not impossible. Because the theft of PII causes enormous trouble for any organization, companies should redouble efforts to protect information assets from the criminal acts of their own employees. Consider the costs to businesses and individuals from the following examples:

- A retailer discovered credit card and other purchasing information had been stolen from customers that had shopped at 103 of its stores. Ironically, information provided by customers who shopped on the company's website was not compromised.[27]

- A bank loses computer backup tapes that held credit card records of 1.2 million government employees. The Department of Defense says that 900,000 of its employees may be affected—including active duty military and civilian contractors. Reports claimed that the tapes also contained information on all 100 U.S. Senators. The tapes went missing while being transported to an off-site storage facility.[28]

- A company that specialized in data collection lost control over 1.6 billion personal records when an individual downloaded and decoded a list of customer passwords.[29]

- A former help desk employee obtained information about more than 30,000 people from his employer—a company that provides software and hardware to businesses that rely on credit reports. According to prosecutors, the identities were used to open fraudulent credit accounts.

ChoicePoint: A Case Study in the Price of PII Mismanagement

One of the most publicized cases of identity theft in recent years was the exposure of thousands of people's PII by thieves who targeted ChoicePoint Inc. The ChoicePoint case generated a lot of media attention, and therefore spurred much debate among legislators and regulators about preventing the loss of personal information. Delving briefly into the facts allows us to learn much about what went wrong and what your organization can do to ensure it avoids the type of incident that plagued ChoicePoint.

ChoicePoint is in the business of selling personal information to businesses for legitimate business reasons. ChoicePoint manages billions of records containing confidential information and/or personal information. Although the details are still coming to light, it appears that ChoicePoint inadvertently sold access to its information to some companies that were formed to gain the PII and either trade in the identities for financial gain or to scam the identities directly. The fraudsters apparently purloined PII about 145,000 people. According to reports, hundreds of the identities have already been subject to ID theft and financial fraud.

The theft of these identities came to light in part because of a law passed in California in 2003, SB 1386. SB 1386 imposed upon organizations with protected personal information of California residents an affirmative duty to disclose to those residents any time their information was improperly provided to, or accessed by, a third party.

After the company disclosed the breach, the Securities and Exchange Commission began looking into sales of company stock (for millions of dollars) made by two executives. The SEC was concerned that the sales were made after ChoicePoint discovered the security breach, but before the breach was made public. ChoicePoint has maintained that the sales were planned before the breach was discovered.[30]

In addition to the SEC investigation, ChoicePoint also is the subject of an FTC probe into how the data wound up in the hands of criminals. ChoicePoint subsequently ceased selling select products to certain small organizations, which is apparently the practice that led to the breach.

Government regulation was not the only price ChoicePoint paid. Investors cared about the breaches, too. ChoicePoint's stock declined double digits in the month following news of the breach. Six months after news of the problem broke, ChoicePoint's stock remained down 10 percent from its value on the day it revealed the loss of the information.

Spyware

Spyware is a hot topic in the tech world, and it's no wonder. Recent studies report a dramatic increase in the amount of spyware being detected on users' machines over the past year. It is estimated that one-third of all computer crashes in 2004 can be traced back to spyware.[32]

Spyware is a broad term for computer code that installs itself on a user's computer to collect information and send it back to the spyware's designer or another party. Similar code, known as adware, collects information on Internet use or shopping habits, making end users an easy target for online marketers who use the information to direct spam emails and other forms of unsolicited advertising. The most malicious forms of spyware can subject its victims to identity theft, barrages of unasked for pop-up ads, hijacked webpages, or redirected searches.

Having spyware on enterprise computers might cause you to lose control of your information. It can also hamper system performance and turn the simplest computing actions into impossible headaches—as in the case of home page hijacking. So how do you protect yourself?

- Keep systems updated. Frequent updates to your software and operating system will help protect your information by fixing known vulnerabilities.

- Scan systems with software tools. Software that's available for purchase or download can be used to identify and eliminate spyware and adware from your computer. Experts suggest using these tools a couple of times a week, depending on your surfing habits.

- Control what employees download. Installing certain programs can sneak spyware or adware onto your system. Only download software if you know what it is—just because it's free doesn't mean you really need it.

Phishing

Phishing involves email or pop-up messages intended to deceive an Internet user into disclosing sensitive PII such as credit card numbers, bank account information, Social Security number, or passwords. A phishing message will typically claim to be from a business that the individual deals with, such as a bank or online payment service. The message will request information it claims is necessary to update or validate account information, for example.

The fake message also might threaten those who do not respond with consequences; for example, customers may be told that if they don't respond with the requested information, their online account access will be deactivated. A typical phishing message will direct individuals to a website that looks nearly identical to a legitimate site, but is actually a forgery run by criminals or criminal organizations. The sole purpose of the site is to trick the victim into divulging his or her personal information so the perpetrators can steal the victim's identity and run up credit card charges, steal from bank accounts, or conduct other criminal activity in that person's name.

Phishing has a relatively high success rate; approximately one out of every seven targets is tricked into providing information such as Social Security, bank account, or credit card numbers.[33] Because any business with an online presence is vulnerable, phishing will continue to have a significant impact, creating huge financial losses and debilitating damage to reputation. An organization's biggest challenge in protecting their customers from phishing is the timing and nature of the fraud. A business may have no idea that its customer has received a fake message, and the customer may provide the information to the scammer in a matter of seconds.

The key to the prevention of a phishing scam today lies primarily in well-informed consumers. Organizations that may be at risk of a phishing attack should take steps to educate their customers about the general existence and nature of these attacks, as well as informing customers of safeguards that will protect against disclosing PII to phishers. When an organization discovers a specific phishing scam, it should take quick action to address the problem. All vulnerable customers should be alerted to the specific scam, and they should be asked to notify the organization if they receive similar messages or any other contact that appears suspicious.

Once alerted to a phishing scam, an organization may be able to put customers' accounts on a watch list, or otherwise protect account information. In light of the continuing threat posed by phishing scams, it might be prudent for businesses to consider advising their customers that they will refrain from ever requesting PII via email. That way, customers know that if they ever get an email requesting such information, it is a scam. Employees should be trained to recognize the warning signs of a phishing campaign, such as customer calls about suspicious-looking emails.

Unfortunately, phishing is not a difficult proposition for the motivated fraudster. In fact, there are a number of websites offering specific instructions on how to create successful phishing campaigns. Some even provide templates to accommodate the effort. Although law enforcement is attempting to crack down on phishers, their efforts are slowed by the ability of the perpetrators to hide in cyberspace. Thus, these scams require careful attention, especially by those working in financial services or other target industries.

Pharming

Another growing online scam is "pharming." Unlike phishing, where the information thief contacts an individual with an email designed to look like an official inquiry form a trusted source, pharming occurs when a scammer is successfully able to divert Web surfers to alternate versions of a website. This is done by actually rerouting traffic on the Internet; the pharmer wrests control of a particular domain name away from the rightful user and instead diverts some Web surfers to a different page. Pharming relies on these misdirected surfers to provide them information they normally would provide only to the official domain.

Several large websites, including a major retail clearinghouse and the foreign page of an auction site, have fallen victim to pharming. It is not clear, however, whether any of these incidents led to the theft of PII. More often, pharming results in inconvenience and frustration because it prevents people from reaching the website they want to visit.

Pharming is expected to increase as pharmers become more sophisticated and are better able to mimic their target websites and lure visitors into disclosing their PII. Vendors can prevent customers from unwittingly disclosing information to pharmers by providing electronic authentication certificates to surfers. Internet providers are also working on defenses that make it harder for pharmers to seize control of the domain name servers that route traffic on the Internet.

Self Assessing: Potential Pitfalls in Managing PII

Now that you've had a chance to review some of the primary concerns for any organization that handles PII, put yourself in the Chief Privacy Officer's place. Which of the following would cause you concern?

1) An employee sends employee medical records via fax instead of email to make sure the records are not intercepted and viewed across the Internet.

2) A company uses a third-party service provider to administer its health plan. Therefore, the company believes, if there is any mistake, it is the service provider's problem.

3) Customers of an online video store agreed, as a condition of membership, to a limitation of liability due to any negligent or intentional acts in the company's managing of the customers' PII. A link on the webpage provides customers with more detail about the agreement—including the small

print, which even prohibits any claim for the company's failure to protect the PII.

4) A company has a policy that prohibits the transmission of any confidential information over email. Employees are allowed to use whatever protection they deem prudent to protect the information.

All of the above scenarios should cause you some concern, for the following reasons:

1) While using a fax machine instead of email may lessen the risk of mass unauthorized distribution, employees commonly misdial telephone and fax numbers. If an employee misdials while transmitting information by fax, a potentially disastrous breach of privacy may occur. Neither fax nor email is a "safe" method of transmission unless greater precautions are taken to ensure the material only reaches authorized recipients.

2) A company's retention of a third party as a data service provider does not necessarily insulate the company from the third party's failure to manage PII properly. Even if legal liability is avoided, other effects—such as loss of consumer confidence and diminished sales or profits—may prove equally harmful to the company's interests.

3) Whether or not a customer signing up online receives sufficient "notice" of the applicable privacy practice remains

unclear. Providing a link to contractual language may not be as good as requiring the customer to review the applicable language before the transaction could be completed. Many merchants instead choose to route all customers onto a "forced path" through the essential terms. Also, if the language denying all liability for privacy mishaps was actually smaller print than the rest of the agreement's language, a court or regulator may conclude that the notice was not "clear and conspicuous," and therefore ineffective.

4) A policy alone is not enough. If the company expects its employees to protect PII over email, or refrain from transmitting unsecured information over open lines, then the company should be specific about what measures should be taken. It is neither practical nor productive to expect employees to secure such data on their own. Nor should the company take the chance that a well-intentioned employee will fail to take the appropriate measures.

Managing Privacy from the Outset

4

The Collection of PII

PII drives commercial enterprises today. Its collection is a priority for an increasingly broad array of businesses in the U.S. and around the world. The manner and purpose for which this data is collected by business is generally beneficial to customers, clients, employees, and businesses alike. Basic PII, including one's name, telephone number, and address is often available to the public—one only needs to consult a phone book or city directory. As we have seen, however, such information is often combined with other data to create a sensitive set of an individual's characteristics—a profile that is far more valuable to business than contact information alone, and one that is more disconcerting to individuals concerned with their privacy. Combined with an unprecedented choice of communications channels and opportunities to contact consumers, the business incentive to collect highly detailed PII is greater than ever.

For decades, offline collection of PII was generally accepted without concern by most consumers. In stores and restaurants, consumers were comfortable supplying credit card numbers. In the past, there was little concern about these transactions, even though a waiter would frequently disappear with one's card for several minutes. In the online world, most reputable businesses protect credit card information at the collection point through use of a secure server or encryption technology, making the transaction perhaps even safer than handing the card over to a stranger in a restaurant. Many consumers, however, remain wary of Internet transactions involving their credit card.

For years, many businesses have retained credit card information long after the initial transaction without consumer knowledge. Privacy concerns have led businesses, and in some cases, legislators, to require that customers be notified of such data collection and retention. More recently, retailers would request—for

What Type of Information Does Your Organization Collect?

Online and offline, businesses enhance the consumer data they collect by combining it with additional information from third party providers. Available information often includes sensitive information. Which of the following types of information does your organization collect? What privacy concerns does this raise?

- Social Security Number
- Date of Birth
- Employee ID Number
- Race
- Ethnicity
- Marital status/Number of children
- Religion
- Political affiliation
- Sexual orientation
- Employment history
- Level of education
- Health information
- Household income
- Financial information such as solvency and creditworthiness
- Home ownership
- Type of automobile owned
- Shopping preferences
- Book preferences
- Music preferences
- Magazine subscriptions
- Hobbies
- Habits, such as smoking or drinking
- Arrest records
- Charitable giving

no reason readily apparent to most consumers—individuals' addresses or zip codes. Often, the consumer would receive catalogs or other direct mailings shortly thereafter.

A 2004 survey of consumers found that respondents are quite willing to share PII with retailers. The percentage of customers willing to disclose the following information is listed below:[34]

- Name   90%
- Mailing address   87%
- Gender   80%
- Email address   79%
- Home phone number   76%
- Date of birth   68%
- Credit Card number   56%
- Interests/Hobbies   46%
- Household income   42%
- Social Security number   18%
- Medical history   6%
- None   5%

It may surprise you to learn that these figures *increased* by 5 to 15 percentage points when the respondents were asked about online retailers.[35] The high level of trust might be partially explained by customers' long-term relationships with many retailers. It could also be attributable to the relatively benign purposes for which this information was generally used. Retailers have shared customer PII with affiliated and unaffiliated third parties for decades; the only obvious result was an increase in catalogs arriving in consumers' mailboxes.

Consumers are often willing to volunteer their PII when a measurable benefit is offered in return, as with the ubiquitous supermarket customer loyalty card. Of course, in exchange for discounts on a selection of items, the consumer is giving the supermarket an abundance of valuable personal information. The public is growing warier of such practices as it learns how the data is being used. Organizations failing to pay attention to these growing business pressures will not only risk losing the ability to collect and use consumer PII, they will risk damage to their reputation and financial well-being.

As an example of the unwelcome scrutiny that can occur in the event of a breach, consider the reaction to news in June 2005 that up to 40 million credit card numbers had been stolen by a hacker. The theft allegedly occurred because of security vulnerabilities at a third-party processor of credit card transactions. After the theft, major credit card companies endured not only the bad publicity stemming from the incident itself, but another wave of criticism from legislators. In a letter to the card companies, U.S. Senator Dianne Feinstein questioned the industry's ability to regulate itself, and highlighted three bills she was sponsoring that would require notification for all similar incidents, impose mandatory standards for the protection of PII, and prohibit the use of certain types of sensitive information.[36]

Collect Only as Much Information as You Truly Need

If information is valuable, then the more information you can get, the better off you are. Right? Not so fast. While it seems counter-intuitive to purposefully collect and retain less information, the possession of PII brings with it a corresponding responsibility to manage it appropriately. Because of the nature of data collection, the volatility of the issue, and the inherent business risks involved, prudent organizations collect the minimum amount of PII necessary to meet business objectives.

Limited collection of PII serves the dual purposes of helping to promote consumer confidence and trust, while reducing risk. It is something "positive" to tell your customers: you not only understand their privacy concerns, you address them by purposely limiting the information you collect from them.

In addition to being an excellent business practice, limited collection of PII is also required under some U.S. and international privacy laws. For example, a key aspect of the Privacy Rule for the Health Insurance Portability and Accountability Act of 1996 is minimum necessary use and disclosure. Organizations subject to HIPAA must make reasonable efforts to collect, use, and disclose the minimum amount of protected health information necessary to achieve the intended purpose of the collection, use, and/or disclosure.[37] The EU Data Protection Directive places similar demands on organizations collecting data on citizens of EU member states. No matter the legal standard, and regardless of the nature of the data, collection of the minimum necessary to accomplish your goals is always a good privacy practice that could help insulate your company from privacy missteps and violations.

Take the Opportunity to Build Trust

Because data collection is your first step in gaining possession of a consumer's PII, it represents your first opportunity to gain that customer's trust. There are several steps you can take at this point:

- Provide notice and be open about your data collection practices. This is the first chance to clearly tell your customer what is being gathered and why it is being gathered. This is particularly important in the online environment, where failure to provide notice of privacy practices could result in violations of state and/or federal laws.

- Tell the consumer whether their PII will be shared with third parties and, if it is, for what purposes.

- On your website, place a conspicuous link to your privacy policy each time PII is requested. Make it easy for website visitors to get informed about your data collection and use.

- Resist the urge to hide your policy in small print at the back of the website. Make it no longer than is necessary (long policies are less likely to be read) and as free of legal terms as possible. Make the print big enough to be easily read.

- Give the consumer a degree of control. Tell them how they can access and update their information, or have it removed from your database.

These simple steps help eliminate consumer confusion, can reduce the risk of consumer complaints and lawsuits, and can keep your organization on the path to managing PII in a responsible and legal manner.

Privacy Laws: General Issues

5

U.S. privacy laws have developed in a patchwork that varies according to industry and state. For example, privacy in financial services is regulated in part by the Gramm-Leach-Bliley Act (also known as the Financial Modernization Act of 1999),[38] along with the Fair Credit Reporting Act[39] and the Fair and Accurate Credit Transactions Act[40], among other laws and regulations. Health-related information is regulated largely by the Privacy Rule of the Health Insurance Portability and Accountability Act.[41] The sending of commercial email messages is regulated by the CAN-SPAM Act.[42] The online collection of information about children is regulated by the Children's Online Privacy Protection Act.[43] These are just a few of the more prominent federal laws controlling various aspects of private sector businesses.

Organizations should monitor privacy-related bills and laws in all jurisdictions in which they do business. This is not an easy task; there is an increasing number of initiatives at the federal, state, and local level. At one point in 2004, the California state legislature was considering more than 20 proposed laws that addressed consumer privacy and the protection of California residents' PII.

The public sector has its own array of laws. The Privacy Act of 1974 provides rules for disclosure of, and personal access to, federal records containing personal information.[44] It regulates the transfer of such information to others, and allows for legal remedies in cases of misuse under the law.

In the meantime, state and federal lawmakers continue to introduce legislation addressing evolving privacy issues, such as identity theft, phishing scams, spyware, and offshore information storage.

Depending upon your industry and the types of PII your organization collects, maintains, and uses, there are a number of privacy laws that likely will apply to you. Several of these laws require your attention regardless of your industry, particularly if you operate a commercial website or send commercial email messages. Chapters 6 through 8 discuss specific laws or bills that you should be aware of. This list is not intended to be comprehensive, but to provide the business manager with a sample of the laws and regulations that impact the way that PII should be managed.

Common Concepts in Privacy Law

Although there are a number of federal laws and regulations that may apply to your organization, and even more state and local provisions, many of these laws use common terms or concepts in controlling PII. Before discussing some of the more frequently applicable statutes, we begin with a quick overview for non-lawyers of the most common concepts: reasonableness, notice, and consent.

Reasonableness

"Reasonableness" is a legal term that can also apply to privacy matters. A number of the laws, regulations, and advisory guidelines that control the use of PII require "reasonable measures" on the part of those collecting, storing, or destroying information. For example, as of June 1, 2005 organizations that use "consumer information" from a credit report are required to take "reasonable measures" to properly dispose of that information when they no longer need it. But what is a "reasonable measure," anyway?

Generally, a reasonable measure is one that is appropriate given the sensitivity of the data involved, the ease with which it could be compromised, and the means available to the party controlling the data. Therefore if your organization has any information from credit reports, it needs to be pulverized, burned, destroyed, etc. so it can't be read or recreated after its use. Merely deleting PII from a computer disk or tape would likely not be viewed as a reasonable precaution, especially because the information is technically there until it is overwritten. If the PII is stored in another type of media,

Data Doesn't Just Disappear When You Hit the "Delete" Key

When the U.S. Veterans Administration donated 139 computers to various schools, state agencies, and thrift stores, it also gave away scores of veterans' medical records and government credit card numbers. The undeleted patient information concerning U.S. veterans included records of patients suffering from psychiatric disorders and AIDS. An Indianapolis reporter discovered the privacy blunder after purchasing three of the donated machines from a local thrift store.[45]

Sounds incredible, right? Not really. A now infamous research study revealed that organizations of all types routinely neglect to protect confidential and sensitive information when tossing out old computers. For those who know how to look for it, old hard drives are a gold mine.

In the study, two MIT graduate students rounded up 158 used hard drives and went to work recovering "deleted" files. They found a treasure trove of medical records, love letters, pornography, and thousands of credit card numbers.[46]

The data they found included:

- Source code from high-tech companies
- Confidential memos
- Internal spreadsheets
- Internal company email
- Financial information from an investment firm
- Transactions, account numbers, and withdrawal amounts from an ATM hard drive
- More than 5,000 credit card numbers from a cash register hard drive[47]

different precautions may be required; what is proper destruction of paper may not be good enough for disks or tapes.

Notice

Notice is a basic component of many privacy laws and regulations facing business today. Notice in the privacy context generally requires informing customers of what you plan to do with their information, their rights, their obligations, and the consequences of their actions. Frequently, notice must include an explanation of how consumers may protect their private information and cancel their permission to share information at a later date.

A good example of a notice required by law is that mandated by the California Online Privacy Protection Act.[48] The Act requires a privacy notice be given to customers of any online organization collecting PII on a resident of California—a requirement that is sweeping in its practical application. Under the law, a conspicuously displayed privacy policy must include:

- the categories of information being collected,

- the categories of third parties with which the information may be shared,

- a description of any mechanism by which a consumer can access his or her PII, and

- a description of the manner by which a consumer will be notified of any changes to the privacy policy.

The law also mandates the manner in which the policy must be posted. Although a number of options are set forth in the law, the posting requirement is satisfied by posting a conspicuous link to its privacy policy on every page on which PII is collected.

As is the case with consent, there are a number of other methods by which notice may be given: by mail, by email, by a click-through page, etc. Some of the laws for privacy transactions govern the time and method by which notice must be given. No matter how your notice is delivered, you should strive to make it easy to find, easy to read, and easy to understand. Some things to keep in mind when drafting your privacy notices:

- Write clearly.

- Use simple language.

- Explain the consequences of the notice.

- Be clear about any action required.

- Point out the significance of the notice and what it means for the holder of the information.

Usually the more lawyerly sounding the language, the tougher it is to understand for the average person, so simplify, simplify, and simplify some more.

Consent

Frequently, privacy laws prohibit the collection or sharing of particular types of information without the consent of the person. What constitutes consent? How is consent expressed? Must it be written? Although each law may have its own specific method of consent, there are a few types of consent that occur repeatedly.

Opting out—Most federal laws in the United States impose an "opt-out" requirement for private information. Under an opt-out approach, a customer is presumed to consent to the sharing of his or her PII; only by taking affirmative action (such as clicking on a link or sending a letter or email) by opting out can he/she prevent his or her PII from being passed around. Not surprisingly, the data suggests that not many people opt out. It has been estimated that only 3% of consumers, given the choice, elect to opt out of information sharing.[49]

Opting In—Unlike opting out, an opt-in choice requires consumer action before information may be shared. In other words, the "default" setting is that data may *not* be shared. The customer must, through deliberate actions, give your company the permission to use their information. This approach is generally consistent with European laws, and not often required by the U.S.

Click-through—Also called "click-wrap," the typical click-through method of consent requires an Internet user to click on a button or graphic to indicate that they agree to the proposed terms of use. Because click-through consent often appears at the bottom of a large portion of text, many users simply click the button rather than actually read the material. This may be one reason why privacy laws have been reluctant to adopt the click-through model as part of their statutory provisions, although these agreements have been upheld in private contract disputes.

The importance of proper notice cannot be overstated. In one case, an online marketer faced a class action lawsuit for its plans to combine information about customers' Web surfing habits (derived from the "cookies" that track visits to particular websites) and PII provided by consumers. As part of the settlement terms for the lawsuit, the company agreed to provide clear notice of its privacy policy, security precautions, and data management to consumers. How much litigation could have been avoided if this path were taken from the start?

Be Careful About Indirect Methods of Consent

When seeking customers' consent, requiring them to take specific actions (such as clicking on a button or checking a box) is the best path. Be careful of other methods, such as suggesting that viewing a page or downloading software indicates consent to be bound by an agreement. An online business discovered this lesson the hard way when a court rejected its argument that a customer had agreed to arbitrate disputes when it downloaded a version of its software. The court found that under the applicable state law, an enforceable contract had not been formed because visitors to the website were not required to view or affirmatively indicate their assent to the license agreement before downloading the software. The court noted that the primary purpose of downloading was to obtain software, not to indicate assent to the terms of a license agreement.[50]

Privacy Laws with a General Impact

6

The Electronic Communications Privacy Act

The ECPA was enacted in 1986 to protect against unauthorized access, interception, or disclosure of private electronic communications by the government, as well as by individuals and third parties. The ECPA prohibits unauthorized "intercepts" of electronic communications, such as email. Part of the ECPA, the Stored Communications Act (SCA), covers electronic communications in storage. The Act provides a cause of action against any person who "intentionally accesses without authorization, a facility through which an electronic communication service is provided and thereby obtains, alters, or prevents authorized access to a wire or electronic communication while it is in electronic storage."[51]

The ECPA has also been interpreted by the courts to give employers the right to monitor employee email, if that email is sent over a system provided by the employer. In a 2003 case from the U.S. Court of Appeals for the Third Circuit, an employer fired an employee after discovering critical emails the employee had sent. The former employee sued, bringing invasion of privacy claims under the ECPA and the SCA. With regard to the ECPA claim, the court decided that because an "interception" of an email can only occur simultaneously with transmission, the employer did not intercept any messages when it retrieved them from storage after they had been sent. The court sided with the employer on the SCA claim as well, because as a nonpublic communications service provider, it was authorized to search emails on its own system.

Although the SCA has been interpreted as allowing employers to search email maintained on their own servers, businesses should provide clear statements of their email monitoring policies to all employees at the time of hire. All new employees should be required to sign an acknowledgement of the policies. Such a practice might help to avoid potential litigation down the road, and also carries the ancillary benefit of creating a more productive work environment. However, monitoring email use of non–US-based employees may not be allowed even if you give them notice so get legal advice BEFORE you take action.

The CAN-SPAM Act

Since its effective date in January of 2004, the "Controlling the Assault of Non-Solicited Pornography and Marketing Act (CAN-SPAM Act)[52] has regulated organizations that use commercial email to communicate with consumers. Congress passed CAN-SPAM in response to public outcry over the amount of commercial email filling people's inboxes on a daily basis. CAN-SPAM applies to any organization sending email for which the "primary purpose is advertising or promoting a commercial product or service."[53] "Transactional" messages, such as emails sent to complete a sale of merchandise or to confirm shipping information, are arguably excluded from most of the Act's requirements.

The Act requires that the "from" line in an email message identify the message's "initiator." By way of a series of fairly complex definitions in the Act, the "initiator" will usually be the advertiser or marketer whose product or service is the subject of the email, as opposed to a middleman who merely transmits the message, such as an email service provider. The purpose of the provision is to make the sender of the message clear to the recipient and eliminate the use of misleading "from" lines that may induce consumers to inadvertently open spam emails. In addition to the "from line" requirements, CAN-SPAM prohibits false or misleading subject lines. Commercial email messages must also include a valid physical postal address for the sender.

Under CAN-SPAM, if your organization is sending out mass email and is covered by the law, your organization must provide a mechanism for recipients to avoid future messages:

- You must inform recipients that they have the option of opting out.

- Each commercial email message must include an opt-out link or valid return email address by which the recipient can request to be removed from future emails.

- The Act also requires that an opt-out mechanism be functioning for at least 30 days after the deployment of the email, and that all opt-out requests are processed and removed from email lists within 10 days of receipt.

CAN-SPAM prohibits selling of an individual's PII after that individual has opted out.

Finally, if an email is unsolicited, meaning that the recipient never gave express consent to receive a message in response to "a clear and conspicuous request for such consent or at recipient's own initiative," then the email must be identified as an advertisement.

Each instance of violating a CAN-SPAM provision is subject to fines of up to $11,000. Additional fines are provided for knowing and willful violations or if the violations include dictionary attacks, address harvesting, or other "aggravating" circumstances."[54] Criminal penalties may also result for certain actions relating to the Act.

In civil actions, damages of up to $250 per message are provided for. A critical point for those implementing PIM programs is that the Act provides that damages may be reduced for inadvertent violations, where the defendant had implemented practices and procedures aimed at preventing violations.[55]

The Telephone Consumer Protection Act

The FCC has amended the Telephone Consumer Protection Act of 1991 to regulate the delivery of facsimile advertisements. Beginning July 1, 2005, it is unlawful to send an unsolicited advertisement to a facsimile machine without the prior written permission of the recipient of the advertisement. Other sections of the law provide:

- The business or entity on whose behalf the fax is being sent must identify itself in the top or bottom margin of each page or on the first page of the fax message, and must include its telephone number and the date and time the fax is sent.

- If a facsimile broadcaster (the person or entity transmitting messages to a fax machine on another person's behalf) demonstrates a "high degree of involvement" in the sender's facsimile messages, such as supplying the facsimile numbers to which a message is sent, the facsimile broadcaster must provide its name on the fax.

- A facsimile broadcaster may be liable if it supplies facsimile numbers to a business or entity sending unlawful fax advertisements.

- Faxes sent to fax servers and personal computers are covered by the faxing rules.

California SB 1386

California has been raising the bar on privacy regulation in recent years. On July 1, 2003, California SB 1386 (often referred to as the California Database Protection Act)[56] took effect, requiring that businesses and nonprofit organizations—regardless of geographic location—must notify California customers if unencrypted personal information maintained in computerized data files has been compromised, or is reasonably believed to have been compromised, by unauthorized access.

Under the law, California consumers must be notified when an unauthorized party obtains certain combinations of their name, Social Security number, driver's license number, account number, credit or debit card number, or security code or password for accessing their financial account. Such incidents have become more common in recent years, as the storage of digital data skyrocketed and the number of potential targets for cyberthieves multiplied.

In 2004, a computer belonging to the University of California was compromised, exposing an estimated 1.4 million individual records that were made available to the university by California's Health and Human Services Agency. The files held personal information on disabled and elderly people who were receiving home care, including individuals' names, addresses, telephone numbers, Social Security numbers, and dates of birth. As a result of the breach, the Health and Human Services Agency recommended that those whose information had been compromised contact the three major credit reporting agencies to place a fraud alert on their credit profiles. They were also advised to be alert for signs of identity theft. However, the Health and Human Services Agency's method of communication was scrutinized by privacy advocates, because the people whose information was put at risk were not contacted individually. Rather, the Agency relied on channels of mass communication of the problem and equally broad warnings to those whose PII was in the compromised database.

Businesses in any state maintaining data on California consumers must be prepared to comply with SB 1386. The best form of compliance of course, is taking preventative steps to ensure that security breaches do not occur in the first place. The University of California example involved a public agency and a state university. Imagine if a similar breach occurred within your organization. How bad would the damage be after you notified more than a million individuals that their information had been compromised, and that it was now up to them to deal with the credit agencies and possible identity theft?

The Cable Communications Policy Act

The Cable Communications Policy Act restricts the use of PII that is stored or collected by cable operators. The law generally prohibits the disclosure of such information, although there are exceptions for governmental investigations, court orders in civil cases, or if a subscriber permits the disclosure.[57]

Complying with Court Orders

Digital security concerns extend beyond California. Consider the case of a federal court in Washington D.C. that was hearing a lawsuit between beneficiaries of trusts held for various Indian Tribes by the Secretary of the Interior. Because much of the evidence involved in the case was stored electronically, the court took the drastic step of quarantining the Department's computers from the Internet:

"It has become abundantly clear in the course of this litigation that the security of Interior's IT systems and the data housed on those systems is of vital interest to the Individual Indian Trust beneficiaries. Indeed, this Court disconnected Interior's IT systems from the Internet in 2001 precisely because the security weaknesses found to exist in those systems threatened the integrity of the Individual Indian Trust data, which data is of immeasurable importance to the beneficiaries for a variety of reasons. Records of transactions involving trust assets, appraisals of trust land, and the progression of ownership of the trust corpus are stored on Interior's IT systems. If this data is corrupted or lost, the beneficiaries will have no way of knowing the value of their trust assets or what the government is doing with those assets."

The Family Educational Rights and Privacy Act

This law applies to PII held by schools and colleges. It allows students to review and challenge mistakes and inaccuracies in their educational records. The law also requires student consent if the institution plans on disclosing the records.[58]

The Real ID Act

In 2005, Congress passed the Real ID Act, which creates a national identification system. The law requires states issuing driver's licenses to incorporate particular features into their cards by the year 2009. The required features include the subject's full legal name, date of birth, address, digital photograph, signature, and an element that is machine-readable, such as a magnetic stripe or chip that can be electronically scanned.[59]

The Real ID Act mainly places limits upon states, not private businesses. It does, however, provide a framework whereby all of the information contained on each card will be available to a number of federal and state offices. Privacy advocates have suggested that the same kinds of security breaches that have plagued private businesses may lead to the theft of the information required under the Real ID Act.[60]

Privacy Laws Affecting Financial Institutions

7

The Fair Credit Reporting Act (FCRA), along with the Gramm-Leach-Bliley Act (GLBA) and the Fair and Accurate Credit Transactions Act (FACT Act), among other things, regulate the manner in which financial institutions can share consumer credit information with affiliates and third parties. These laws also set forth specific security obligations for organizations collecting, storing, and using consumers' non-public financial information.

Gramm-Leach-Bliley

In essence, Title V (the Title addressing privacy issues) of GLBA requires clear disclosure by all financial institutions of their policies with regard to the sharing of non-public personal information with affiliated and non-affiliated third parties. The Act also requires that individuals be given an opportunity to opt-out of the sharing of their non-public personal information with nonaffiliated third parties, subject to a few limited exceptions. Securities and Exchange Commission Regulation S-P mirrors the GLBA, but applies the law to broker-dealers, registered investment advisors and investment companies.

Under GLBA, only an institution that is "significantly engaged" in financial activities is considered a financial institution. This may include organizations that extend credit to consumers, such as banks and credit unions and securities brokers, but could also include companies that one might not, at first blush, think of as a financial services organization. Payday lenders, check-cashing businesses, professional tax preparers, auto dealers engaged in financing or leasing, electronic funds transfer networks, mortgage brokers, credit counselors, real estate settlement companies, and retailers that issue credit cards to customers could be covered by GLBA.

GLBA does not just apply to information about individuals with whom your organization does business. It regulates the dissemination of the non-public personal information of both "consumers" and "customers." According to the law, a "consumer" is any person seeking to obtain, or who has obtained, a financial product or service from a bank for personal, family, or household purposes. A loan applicant appears to meet this definition, and thus would likely be covered by the law. A "customer" is a consumer who has a continuing relationship with the financial institution, such as an individual who has opened a credit card account. The distinction between customers and consumers is important, because under GLBA consumers are generally entitled to a privacy notice only if the institution will share the consumer's information with an unaffiliated third party. A customer, on the other hand, must receive a privacy notice, regardless of whether the financial institutions shares information with third parties. This notice must be delivered when the customer relationship is established (for example, when a consumer opens a credit card account) and at least once a year as long as the relationship lasts.

GLBA generally requires the following kinds of information to be included in a privacy notice:

- The categories of personal information collected

- The categories of personal information disclosed to other parties

- The categories of affiliates and nonaffiliated third parties to which information is disclosed

- An explanation of the right to opt-out of disclosures to non-affiliated third parties

- A description of the type of disclosures to nonaffiliated parties that are exceptions to the rule and don't carry the right to opt-out

- An explanation of the ability to opt-out of disclosures of information among affiliates under FCRA

- If information is disclosed to third parties to conduct marketing campaigns on behalf of the financial institution, a separate statement of the categories of information disclosed and the categories of third parties to whom the information will be disclosed

- A description of confidentiality and security policies and practices

- Categories of personal information about former customers that are disclosed, and to whom such information is disclosed

- Delivery of the initial privacy notice before the financial institution discloses any personal information to a non-affiliated third party

The GLBA provides a number of exceptions to its notice and opt-out requirements. It does not, for example, give individuals the right to opt-out of the financial institution's sharing of information with outside companies that provide essential services, like data processing or account servicing. Nor does it require that opt-out rights be given where disclosure is made to outside service providers that market the financial company's products or services.

In instances where notice is provided and an individual chooses not to opt-out, a recipient of that individual's financial information remains bound by the privacy policy of the disclosing financial institution. Thus, the recipient may use the information for its own purposes or re-disclose it to a third party, but only in a manner consistent with the financial institution's privacy notice.

The Fair Credit Reporting Act (FCRA) and the Fair and Accurate Credit Transactions Act (FACT) Act

Consumer credit reports are used for a variety of reasons by a wide variety of organizations. A credit report can be defined as any communication of information by a consumer reporting agency that bears on a consumer's credit worthiness, standing, capacity, personal character, general reputation, standard of living, or other characteristics, which is used in establishing the consumer's eligibility for credit, insurance, employment, or other permissible purposes.[61] FCRA limits the use of the credit report for the following specified and limited purposes:

- Applications for credit, insurance, and rentals for personal, family, or household purposes

- Employment, including hiring, promotion, reassignment, or retention (A credit reporting agency may not release a credit report for employment decisions without consent.)

- Court orders, including grand jury subpoenas

- Legitimate business needs in transactions initiated by the consumer for personal, family, or household purposes

- Account review (Periodically, banks and other companies review credit files to determine whether they wish to retain the individual as a customer.)

- Professional licensing

- Child support payment determinations

- Law enforcement access

FCRA generally permits the sharing of credit transaction and history information among "corporate affiliates" without notification. (Interestingly, the term is not defined by FCRA.) Sharing of this information with non-affiliates, however, generally requires the organization to provide "notice" of the policy and give recipients the opportunity to restrict the sharing of their information.

FCRA generally prohibits the use of credit reports for "target marketing," which has been the subject of a good deal of debate and litigation. In one well-known case, a credit reporting agency unsuccessfully attempted to challenge the prohibition. The court determined, however, that the name, address, date of birth, telephone number, Social Security number, account type, opening date of account, credit limit, account status, and payment history of a consumer could not be sold for marketing purposes because they constituted a "credit report" under FCRA.

In addition to FCRA, some states have passed their own laws governing the use of financial information. Some of these laws provide greater protection to consumers than that provided by FCRA and the FACT Act.

Financial services laws set forth specific rules for the handling of consumer and customer data. They are complex, and separate statutes often impose overlapping requirements. The proper method for handling data may depend upon the specific type of data that is involved.

The FACT Act amended parts of the FCRA to help combat the threat of identity theft. The FACT Act authorizes consumers to obtain free copies of their credit reports, to place a "fraud alert" on their credit reports, and to correct inaccurate information. The FACT Act also contains provisions that will go into effect in the future that limit merchants' use of full account numbers on receipts.

The Right to Financial Privacy Act and Bank Secrecy Act

These two laws govern the privacy bank customers have in their account information. The Right to Financial Privacy Act (RFPA) limits the federal government's ability to obtain customer records from a wide variety of financial institutions, including not only traditional banks but also businesses such as money services businesses, casinos, and travelers check issuers. Unless an exception applies, if the government requests information

Disposing of Data

Businesses or individuals that have consumer information (including paper and electronic records) from credit reports may be under a new obligation to properly destroy the information when it is no longer needed. As of June 1, 2005, the Federal Trade Commission requires that the information be properly disposed of to help combat financial crimes and identity theft. Although the rule does not specify the methods that will satisfy its requirement of "reasonable measures" to dispose of PII, at a minimum even small businesses should plan on shredding any paper records containing credit report information. Larger businesses may want to use a document disposal company.

about a customer, the bank must notify the customer of the request and allow the customer time to challenge the government's request.[62]

One of the exceptions to the RFPA, however, is reports that financial institutions are required to file pursuant to the Bank Secrecy Act (BSA). The BSA requires a bank to report suspicious activity. Suspicious activity includes insider trading, transactions of more than $5,000 that appear related to illegal activity, and any cash transfer of more than $10,000.[63]

HIPAA

8

Overview

The Health Insurance Portability and Accountability Act (HIPAA) generally governs health care providers that have private health information. It also governs employee health plans and health care clearinghouses. The HIPAA Privacy Rule is intended to protect "individually identifiable health information" and places a number of obligations on "covered entities." These include:

- Notifying patients about their privacy rights and permissible uses of their individually identifiable health information

- Adopting and implementing privacy procedures

- Training employees so that they understand the privacy procedures

- Designating an individual to oversee the implementation and compliance with the privacy procedures

- Securing patient records containing individually identifiable health information so that they are not readily available to those who do not need them

The HIPAA Privacy Rule also generally requires an individual's written authorization before his or her protected health information can be used or disclosed.

At its core, the HIPAA Privacy Rule places restrictions on covered entities with regard to their use of patients' personal information. However, it also places restrictions on "business associates" of these entities. These business associates may include direct and Internet marketers, pharmaceutical manufacturers, medical equipment providers, database vendors, and a host of other vendors and contractors who may use PII. The Rule requires covered entities to include specific provisions in their agreements with business associates that safeguard protected health information, and addresses permissible ways that covered entities may share this information with business associates. One of the areas of the law that has garnered a lot of attention from American businesses is the use of individually identifiable health information for marketing purposes. The Act defines marketing as "a communication about a product or service that encourages recipients of the communication to purchase or use the product or service."[64] HIPAA places significant limitations on disclosure of protected health information to business associates (such as marketers) without consent and, when disclosure is allowed, it places restrictions on the use of such information.

HIPAA and Your Health Plan

If your organization offers group health insurance to employees, HIPAA's Privacy Rule may require special measures to protect employee health information, including medical records and payment information. The Rule may require the creation of an "information blockade" that prevents employee health information from going beyond the office of the plan administrator (most likely human resources/benefits personnel). The Rule prohibits the plan administrator from disclosing health-related information to the employer for purposes of hiring, promotion, reassignment, or termination. Some of the safeguards that need to be implemented by employers include:

- Reviewing and limiting the flow of protected health information throughout the organization

- Minimizing the number of people with access to protected health information

- Requiring passwords to access certain electronic files containing protected health information

- Assignment of a Privacy Officer who will ensure that the health plan complies with the regulations (This job function can be filled by an existing employee, such as a human resources manager.)

- Appropriate employee training for any employee who must handle protected health information to perform his or her duties

The Department of Health and Human Services' Office of Civil Rights—which has enforcement powers under HIPAA—receives about 100 complaints a week. Most of these complaints involve impermissible use or disclosure of health information, lack of adequate safeguards to protect information, refusal or failure to provide access to information, disclosure of more information than is necessary, and inadequate authorization for disclosure. Criminal penalties for "wanton disregard" of the Privacy Rule include up to 10 years in prison and $250,000 fines. In one recent criminal prosecution for violation of HIPAA, an employee of a Seattle cancer treatment organization was sentenced to 16 months in prison and ordered to pay a $9,000 fine for stealing the personally identifiable health information of a patient. The employee used the patient's name, date of birth, and Social Security number to obtain credit cards and make thousands of dollars in purchases. Although the prosecutor in the case recommended only 12 months in prison, the judge cited the "vicious attack on someone fighting for his life" and added 4 additional months.

Another part of HIPAA, the Security Rule, recently went into effect for most businesses. (Small health plans have until 2006 to comply.) The Security Rule governs health-related PII that is in electronic form. The Security Rule requires that this electronic PII be protected by reasonable administrative, physical, and technical safeguards.[65] The Security Rule contains a number of precise requirements; if your business uses or maintains health-related records, you and your counsel should be sure you understand the Security Rule's requirements.

Online Doctor's Visits Increase as Privacy Concerns Are Addressed

Internet "house calls" from physicians are becoming attractive to patients and businesses, now that a new study has revealed the potential cost savings available to insurers.[66] Online house calls provide patients with non-critical health care in a faster, cheaper, and more convenient way than the traditional visit to your doctor's office. Benefits to patients include the availability of online prescriptions or lab results and increased communication with physicians.

Despite these promises, the medical community balked at online patient care because of privacy concerns, among other things. Now new secure messaging tools are helping overcome these fears, giving healthcare institutions the ability to protect personally identifiable medical and insurance information to meet HIPAA demands while providing patients with greater access to care.[67]

PIM Compliance

9

In an electronic business environment inundated with PII, a management system that ensures legal compliance, meets business needs, and effectively manages risk is a business necessity. A comprehensive, enterprise-wide PIM program will help meet those objectives, but only if it is implemented in a professional manner by individuals dedicated to its success.

Compliance can be defined as acting "in accordance with any accepted standard or criteria."[68] In the privacy context, these "accepted standards" almost universally include a combination of the following:

- **Laws**—Know the statutes, foreign and domestic, that apply to your organization based on the types of data it collects.

- **Industry standards**—Generally accepted standards, such as the use of Secure Sockets Layer (SSL) for transmitting credit card numbers, for example, should be met, if not exceeded.

- **Consumer advocacy group guidelines**—Keep up with these groups and their recommendations because they may seek to enforce privacy promises and standards through the courts.

- **Industry groups/trade association requirements**—Often, your business may have to meet certain qualifications to retain its membership in a particular group.

Determining your Compliance Criteria

PII compliance criteria set the stage for your PIM program. They give you guidance on how your organization should collect, maintain, use, manage, and/or share PII with third parties. Monitoring of these criteria is not one person's job; the responsibility should flow from the privacy officer (or other designated executive) down to individual department heads whose job duties include the use of PII. Staff with responsibility for handling PII must be encouraged to monitor the sources of privacy criteria for any changes or developments. Determining which criteria must be met, and by which departments, is challenging—especially if your organization has more than one line of business. That said, legal standards should always be your starting point, as failure to comply with the law likely carries the greatest risk for your organization.

Privacy Compliance Criteria Evolve— So Stay on Top of Changes

It is no small matter to keep up with the laws, regulations, industry standards, and best practices that deal with privacy. Your privacy program should be designed to keep up with changes in the rules as they become known. Thus, your PIM program—and more specifically, the privacy compliance criteria that drive your program—requires continuous monitoring and adjustment.

To stay on top of privacy management best practices and the new privacy laws, your organization should:

- Conduct an initial privacy audit to determine the privacy criteria that apply to each branch of business in your organization and what privacy practices are already in place (if any)

- Develop organizational goals and objectives to deal with the wide variety of privacy related issues affecting your organization

- Review privacy laws that affect your industry and your organization

- Monitor new state, federal, and local legislation addressing privacy

- Develop privacy practices and written policies that meet legal requirements and organizational objectives

- Conduct a gap analysis to expose any gaps between existing privacy management practices and new or updated practices and policies

- Implement and update privacy practices and policies

- Conduct training, education, and monitoring

Remember: like most information management activities, managing private information is a process, not a project. After the privacy program is established, it will require ongoing management and updating to address changes in your business and domestic and international laws.

In addition to remembering to include all divisions, any successful PIM strategy requires considering those connected to your business: your contractors, your vendors, and your customers. The failure to anticipate their use of data in your possession, or their concern for their own PII, could lead to costly headaches.

When It Comes to Privacy Your Business Relationships Can Impact Your Organization

Consider the following real life examples:

- A technology company in Chicago is affected when PII of about 30,000 workers is stolen from computers at an HR outsource vendor of the technology company.
- Tapes containing data about 600,000 customers are exposed when a courier company loses the box containing the information.
- Weak security at a third-party vendor may have exposed 40 million identities of a credit card company's customers.
- A travel company used by the Department of Justice had a computer stolen that contained personal information of 80,000 employees.
- Loss of tapes by another package delivery service exposed 120,000 Department of Defense employees and their identities.

part II

Developing a Successful Privacy Information Management (PIM) Program

Building Your PIM Program | 10

Now that you are familiar with the basic privacy issues facing modern business, it's time to get to work. Whether your organization already has a privacy policy, or whether it is building one from scratch, you must be ready to implement a comprehensive system that will protect your company from data loss, angry customers, plaintiffs' attorneys, and government regulators.

This is a daunting task. Fortunately, this book can help, no matter where your privacy practices are. This part of the book provides step-by-step guidance on how to engage your organization, formulate an effective policy, implement the policy, monitor compliance, find and address violations, and improve your practices as the law—and customers' expectations—change.

Naturally, this book cannot address the individual needs and specific requirements of every organization. Nor can this book prescribe specific products or services, for two reasons. First, the products or services your business needs may differ from those another business needs. Second, technology constantly improves and presents new solutions for data security. Any list of software or hardware solutions would be obsolete shortly after it was created.

Rather than providing you with a shopping list, our approach will allow you to incorporate new technology and revisit your policy as your business changes and grows. This approach draws upon the concept of Information Management Compliance, a method developed to help organizations meet their information management goals.

Information Management Compliance and Privacy

In an electronic business environment inundated with PII, a management system that ensures legal compliance, meets business needs, and effectively manages risk is a business necessity.

A comprehensive, enterprise-wide PIM program will help meet those objectives, but only if it is implemented in a professional manner by individuals dedicated to its success.

In a previous book, *Information Nation,* written by Randolph A. Kahn and Barclay T. Blair, a compliance methodology to manage information-related activities was introduced.[69] This methodology, called "Information Management Compliance," brings compliance, business, and technological considerations to bear on the management of information. The concepts of Information Management Compliance can also be applied to the management of PII.

Drawing on this approach, the next chapters cover the basics, from beginning to end, of implementing an effective PIM program.

- **Getting Everybody On Board**—Effective PIM requires the commitment and involvement of everybody in your organization: the executives who control the budget, the managers who oversee data collection and use, IT professionals who protect the data, and the employees whose jobs give them access and control over PII.

- **Assessing Your PIM Needs**—Before you can establish an effective policy, you must determine how your organization gathers, uses, and stores PII. You must determine what types of PII you collect. You must analyze your relationships with third parties and how they use PII. A comprehensive privacy audit will answer these questions and prepare you for the next step.

- **Formulating Privacy Principles, Policies, and Guidelines**—Establishing the principles that will guide your organization's PIM strategy is a cooperative effort. You must consider the legal requirements, but these only serve as a starting point. A properly drafted privacy policy will give potential customers confidence and benefit your organization's bottom line. Guidelines will give employees implementable steps that will keep the organization in line with the policies.

- **Implementing the Policy and Procedures**—Implementation is a deliberate process. Before anything changes, you need to evaluate whether this new approach will meet the organization's needs. Rollout of the plan will require training, education, and support from all levels of the organization.

- **Monitoring Compliance**—Once your PIM policies and processes are up and running, your organization must be vigilant to see they are complied with. Employees must understand the reasons why they are expected to comply with the policies and they must understand the consequences of failure.

- **Enforcing Violations**—Consistent and serious enforcement is necessary to any successful PIM effort. Enforcement will encourage employees to follow the directives, will establish that your company is serious about privacy, and will help you realize weaknesses in your system that can be fixed with better policies, better training, or better technology.

- **Improving Your Policy**—Because of the shifting privacy landscape, where each day brings new laws, new regulations, and new court decisions affecting businesses that work with PII, your policy must change to meet legal and consumer demands.

Bringing Everybody on Board

11

One of the overriding essentials of the development of an effective PIM program is to gain the active participation of all levels of the organization, especially senior management. Unless you have the executive support for your privacy initiative, it will not be as successful as it needs to be. Executive participation is important because company officers set the company's agenda and control the budgets, priorities, and employees. They must support the organization's privacy strategy.

Active participation and leadership from CEOs, presidents, and/or executive directors is critical to getting a PIM program launched. This is true even in organizations with an executive-level Chief Privacy Officer. In order to be handled effectively, PIM must flow from the top down. Experience shows that without executive-level leadership, privacy initiatives are likely to fail. Perhaps most important is the need to send a clear message to all employees that privacy is a top priority for our customers, and therefore it is a strategic interest to our organization. High-level direction of PIM initiatives is necessary to achieve the following goals:

- **Enterprise-wide buy in**—This is necessary to assure consistency in the development of, implementation of, and compliance with PIM initiatives. Remember that employees may see themselves as being accountable only to their immediate supervisors. It is important that they realize that privacy requirements and goals go beyond their departmental obligations.

- **Budgetary authority for funding PIM programs and initiatives**—Departmental managers may be reluctant to allocate resources to an initiative which, on its surface, appears to have little bottom line benefit to their department. These managers must be given the resources and the marching orders that will advance PIM development and implementation.

- **Setting organizational PIM objectives**—Because PIM must transcend departmental mentality, executive support will go a long way toward ensuring that privacy goals are met and the organization's privacy policies are adhered to at all levels.

- **Delegation, oversight, and influence over PIM initiatives**—The executive will set the privacy initiatives in motion, but he or she must depend on departmental managers to develop and implement the PIM program. Active oversight and direction is critical once the responsibility has been delegated. Those lower on the organizational chain should know that the executives are watching.

- **Accountability for privacy successes and failures**—Accountability for privacy at the executive level sends a message to employees, consumers, regulatory agencies, and shareholders that privacy is important to the organization. This will positively impact both the risk management and bottom line results of the PIM initiatives.

Active and consistent executive leadership in PIM efforts will contribute to privacy awareness and ensure an organization's compliance with and responsible practice of PIM.

Enterprise-wide Buy-in and Consistency

The importance of a comprehensive PIM program cannot be overstated in today's environment of increased regulation, scrutiny from consumer watchdog groups, and a sharp focus on privacy from the plaintiff's bar. Executive leadership is one element necessary to ensure serious attention to the privacy issue throughout the enterprise—to each of the employees who handle personal information on a regular basis. It is those individuals who put PIM concepts into action. Your employees will either improve consumer trust, reduce business risk, and eliminate executive-level exposure to personal liability; or they will land the organization in a morass of privacy problems. These individuals must understand the commitment and investment that your organization has made to PIM. Those executives and managers overseeing your policy should deliver a regular, consistent message throughout the organization that PIM demands careful attention every day.

For businesses that have divisions that operate independently of one another, PIM leadership is even more crucial. This is particu-

Another FBI Top 10

Reviewing the FBI's top 10 priorities makes you realize the priority that law enforcement places on protecting information, including personal information.

1. Protect the United States from terrorist attack.
2. Protect the United States against foreign intelligence operations and espionage.
3. Protect the United States against cyber-based attacks and high-technology crimes.
4. Combat public corruption at all levels.
5. Protect civil rights.
6. Combat transnational and national criminal organizations and enterprises.
7. Combat major white-collar crime.
8. Combat significant violent crime.
9. Support federal, state, county, municipal, and international partners.
10. Upgrade technology to successfully perform the FBI's mission.

larly true if separate business divisions share consumer PII. Many privacy laws require unified privacy and security procedures across business divisions. For example, the Gramm-Leach-Bliley Act sets forth specific requirements for financial services organizations that share PII with their affiliates. Properly managing PII is sufficiently difficult within independent organizations; ensuring consistent performance among separate business divisions increases the challenge. Because lines of communication in such organizations often begin and end within each individual division, somebody at the executive level must take the lead and take responsibility for monitoring compliance. With active participation from the company's front office, businesses have a much greater likelihood of maintaining cohesive PIM practices that meet business needs and legal requirements.

Authorizing PIM Expenditures

One of the most serious challenges in getting a successful PIM program launched is gaining commitment for the funding of its development and implementation. When it comes to PIM, money talks. The development, implementation, and upkeep of an effective PIM program will require investments from each department that handles PII. These costs can arise from a variety of sources: purchasing new locking file cabinets, making workspaces more secure, and investments in privacy and security management software. Substantial investment may be necessary on the front end in order to inventory your PII, determine applicable laws, and develop policies and appropriate procedures. Because PIM is likely a relatively new business imperative, many organizations have not found a regular spot for PIM in the annual budget. Many people assume that a privacy budget belongs in the IT department, since IT is in charge of electronic security and storage. Others will argue that because privacy is driven first and foremost by legal requirements, the budget should lie within the legal department. Although each of these views is valid, neither considers the true scope and expenses of implementing a successful PIM program.

Because of the perceptions (and misperceptions) regarding the funding of a PIM program, managers of independent departments or business units are often reluctant to spend any of their department's budget on these efforts. After all, division heads are often evaluated based on their division's return, and the active management of privacy does not immediately contribute measurable returns to a division's bottom line. Executives, therefore, must either give departmental leaders a designated budget for the PIM initiative or direct these individuals to make the necessary allocations. Optimally, the CEO—with likely input from the CFO—may want to consider creating an entirely independent budget line for organization-wide PIM programs. Under this approach, each department can pull necessary funds for development and implementation of its portion of the enterprise-wide PIM program. This strategy will tend to reduce or eliminate resistance based on manager concerns over departmental profit and loss.

Setting Corporate Goals

The participation of all levels of the enterprise is essential to set enterprise-wide privacy goals and objectives. This process should be driven from the executive level, with the inclusion of the company president, CEO, CFO, or CPO (if such a position exists within the organization). Other people may be included in the development of these goals, but bear in mind that involving PIM team members from individual departments may carry the risk of bias. Whoever ultimately works on the goals, their mission is to determine the needs for the collection and use of PII, as well as the corresponding levels of privacy protections required by applicable laws and professional standards, as well as setting objectives for transparency and consumer friendliness. They will need to balance the benefits and risks of the collection and use of consumer data, giving special weight to digital data, which is at the center of current privacy concerns. The process should be undertaken with the understanding that corporate goals and privacy compliance criteria may not always match up perfectly. In such instances, the team must carefully analyze the risk in order to determine the best direction for the organization.

The chief executive participating in the setting of corporate goals has the unique ability to view critical PIM issues from a 30,000-foot level. In other words, he or she is free from a department-centric mindset that may inhibit the ability of division managers. In many cases, department heads have their own immediate bottom lines in mind. The establishment of goals requires an appreciation of the value of proper PIM to the organization as a whole, over the long term.

Delegation, Oversight, and Influence

While executive participation is required for origination of PIM policies and practices, the implementation of these processes will be handled by middle-level management. Executives must ensure that responsibility for PIM tasks is delegated to the proper managers. These managers will be responsible for implementing PIM processes in their departments, training their staffs, and enforcing the new rules.

Those overseeing the PIM program must keep in mind the seriousness of the delegated responsibilities and ensure that the individuals assigned these responsibilities will give them the appropriate level of focus. Remember: violations of privacy laws and internal policies can have disastrous effects for your organization. Your firm's PIM plan should be left in the hands of managers who have demonstrated the ability to execute critical business tasks. Managers must fully understand the goals of the PIM program and how these objectives apply to their departments. Managers also should be extensively briefed on the risks involved in the mismanagement of PII. Individuals will take privacy more seriously if they understand the immediate risks, as opposed to the long-term benefits.

Once PIM has been delegated to the appropriate managers, the executive should still offer input as needed. The executive officers must oversee the process of PIM. Not only does this ensure proper development and implementation of PIM processes, it sends an important message to the public, regulatory agencies, and shareholders: privacy is being taken seriously at the highest levels of the organization. Staff will be far more likely to buy into the new procedures when they are actively and vocally supported by the company's executives. Executive involvement may range from attendance at departmental meetings, to frequent memos, to company-wide seminars on the topic of privacy. The proper channel by which company brass demonstrates its commitment to PIM depends on the organizational culture. Whichever channel is best for your organization, the message will get through. Even as the executive role in PIM may gradually change, it should never be eliminated. In fact, executive involvement will increase from time to time during annual privacy audits and periods of risk analysis.

Accountability and Liability

In this era of privacy, consumers, regulators, and legislators want assurances from upper-tier management that PII and other confidential information is being managed in a legal and ethical manner. This concern is reflected not only in specific privacy laws, but in a wider movement for executive accountability. Corporate scandals and resulting laws, such as Sarbanes-Oxley, have put a tremendous amount of pressure on business executives to be accountable for the information their organizations maintain, among other things. Failure to handle private and confidential information correctly could result in personal liability at the executive level or on the organization for which they have stewardship. The post-Enron atmosphere has made it incumbent upon executives to know what information the organization collects, by what means, how it is maintained, whether it is shared with third parties, and the means by which information is transmitted.

Of course, many of the privacy-specific laws provide for individual accountability as well. The HIPAA Privacy Rule, for example, has provisions calling for steep monetary penalties as well as significant jail time for offenses committed with the intent to sell, transfer, or use individually identifiable health information for commercial advantage, personal gain, or malicious harm.

You may recall discussion in chapter 5 of a nationally recognized online marketing company and its legal entanglements as a result of its plan to combine information gathered via cookies on the Internet with personal information maintained by a company which it had recently acquired. Just prior to the acquisition and the FTC investigation and lawsuits by 10 states that followed, shares of the online marketing company were trading at approximately $135 per share. During the period of the lawsuits and investigation, share values slid precipitously. By the time the lawsuits and investigation were brought to their conclusions, shares had fallen in value by nearly $100 per share, setting the company's principals and shareholders back millions of dollars.

It is absolutely necessary that executives remember that safeguarding PII is not just a matter of being a good corporate citizen. The integrity of this information has direct and dramatic impact on the financial well being of the business and individual shareholders.

The Gramm-Leach-Bliley Act provides similar penalties for business people who do not adequately protect consumers' personal financial information. Aside from the obvious legal ramifications and long-term harm to reputation, the executive might also risk substantial personal loss as a shareholder.

Creating a Culture of PIM Awareness

The success of a PIM program depends upon a pervasive culture of privacy within an organization. The development of this culture requires cooperative involvement from executives and middle managers who can communicate, train, and monitor all employees. Personal presentations, email notices, Intranet postings, and policy memos can drive home the point: privacy is paramount.

A CEO statement addressing the importance of privacy and the PIM program is an excellent first step in creating a positive culture. The CEO statement must, of course, be distributed to all existing employees. It should be made part of new employee orientation materials and become a standard component of any organization-wide employee handbook. It might be useful to have new employees sign an acknowledgement that they have read and understand the CEO's statement, and that they will adhere to the PIM practices of the organization. CEO statements on privacy and PIM should address topics such as the following:

- PII is an asset that the company relies upon to conduct a profitable business.

- PIM is a high priority for consumers and customers, and it carries risks for the organization that can have both positive and negative effects on the organization's bottom line and shareholder value.

- The company seeks to comply with all privacy laws and maintaining compliance is dependent on the conduct of all employees.

- Each employee will receive PIM training.

- The company conducts ongoing PIM monitoring.

- Failure to comply with PIM practices and policies may lead to discipline, up to and including termination.

By communicating the critical nature of privacy compliance to all staff from the outset, the CEO is setting the tone for an environment of privacy awareness. This awareness will endure through the comings and goings of employees at all levels.

The PIM Team

Following the determination and assignment of executive leadership for the development and life cycle of the PIM program, the executive must assemble the PIM Team. The team will typically be comprised of senior-level managers who head work groups that collect, use, or maintain PII, among others with an interest or expertise in the issue. This team will oversee the development, implementation, and operation of the PIM processes, so it is critical that each team member is carefully selected. Team members should be able to contribute to the development of the PIM plan, and lead its implementation and subsequent monitoring. Because this team will exist throughout the lifespan of a PIM program, those selecting its members should take into account the likelihood of the employee's continued service. Keep in mind likely successors who could fill the void if or when team members transition to new areas.

In a typical large organization, the team would likely include representation from the following departments:

- Legal
- IT
- Marketing
- Sales
- Human Resources
- Customer Service
- Data Processing

Depending on your organizational structure and industry, the team may also include individuals representing:

- Risk Management
- Records Management
- Compliance

Of course, other departments should be included as deemed necessary by the executive in charge.

The executive heading up the PIM program will lead the team through the initial stages of setting corporate goals and assigning necessary tasks, such as documenting of information collection and use practices of all company departments. More importantly, the senior executive will convey to the PIM team the particular privacy issues facing the organization and why they are critical to the company's success. The executive representative must lead the discussions about balancing of consumer privacy concerns and legal requirements against the needs of the organization to gather and use PII. These discussions will help each team member set departmental goals that advance the organization's overall privacy goals.

Once the PIM Team has a solid grasp of the goals and objectives it is to accomplish, it must be empowered to make contributions and decisions about privacy. This is, after all, the team which will drive the direction of PIM on a divisional and enterprise-wide basis. Although executives need to guide the team and set the agenda, formation of the plan should come from the team itself.

Executive Checklist—The Essentials for Effective PIM Leadership

- Identify key players and personally communicate to them their involvement in the PIM Team.
- Understand the applicable privacy laws and industry practices. Communicate them to your PIM Team.
- Retain budget authority or assign it to the CFO or CPO.
- Drive the development of PIM processes with one eye on legal requirements and one eye on business necessities.
- Communicate your support of PIM processes across the enterprise through use of multi-channel employee communications.
- Leave no doubt that PIM is a business imperative which all staff must understand and participate in according to organizational practices and policies.

Assess Your PIM Needs

12

Conducting the Privacy Audit

Before you can draft policies, guidelines, and procedures for effective PIM, you need to know exactly what information your organization needs to protect. One of the PIM team's first tasks will be to conduct a privacy audit. This will identify the types of PII you collect, maintain, and use. It also will track the flow of that data into, within, and outside your organization. The audit also serves to uncover—and allow for the correction of gaps between any existing privacy practices and policies you have in place and applicable privacy laws.

The precise nature of the privacy audit will depend on whether it is being conducted as part of the initial PIM program development or is being conducted as part of an ongoing PIM program. Whatever the case, a thorough audit can be long and sometimes painstaking. It is, however, essential to creating effective PIM policies and procedures. The privacy audit also represents a critical step in building trust with potential and existing customers.

Whether conducted internally or by a professional auditing firm, the auditing process requires considerable access to the information collected throughout the organization and those who collect the PII or enable the collection. The auditors will need to conduct detailed interviews with managers or heads of departments that use PII. Before you begin the audit, the PIM team must notify those who need to be interviewed and secure their cooperation. An incomplete or poorly conducted audit serves only to create a false sense of security. When this is subsequently shattered by a violation of policies or a data breach that could have been prevented from the outset, your organization and its shareholders will pay a price that could greatly exceed the cost of doing it right from the outset.

Gathering a PII Inventory

The initial step in the privacy audit is also the most critical in the PIM process: the gathering of an inventory of the organization's existing PII, along with any written policies and procedures that govern the handling of this information. Failure to account for all PII during the inventory will result in holes in the PIM program. The audit should break down your organization's PII by type or category of data (e.g., financial, health-related, data collected from children, etc.) so that all controlling rules and standards can be identified. During this process, those conducting the inventory should conduct interviews to identify PII and confidential business information on all media, including hard paper copies, network computers, laptop computers, personal digital assistants, even digital photocopiers (as we learned in chapter 3). The auditors should also assess PII that is collected and stored online or in the custody of a third party. If desired, your organization may conduct a simultaneous inventory audit of other confidential business information that must be safeguarded under other recent corporate governance laws, such as Sarbanes-Oxley.

Aside from the inventory of the PII itself, this process must also include the gathering of any contracts with third parties or affiliates that authorize the sharing or transfer of PII to those third parties. These contracts should be reviewed during the subsequent gap analysis to ensure that all third parties who receive PII in your organization meet or exceed the privacy standards imposed by your PIM program. The auditors also should review any existing data retention policies, which may provide insight on how to eliminate old data that is no longer needed by the organization.

Contractors Can Create Problems

One recent story in the news involved a security breach on the website of a payroll services provider. According to news reports the W2 records of more than 25,000 individuals may have been exposed.[70]

Who handles your W2 records? Are you confident in their PII protection?

The areas of most business organizations that would likely have or use PII include:

- Legal
- HR
- Finance
- Tax
- IT
- Security
- Marketing
- Sales
- Customer service

Other potential business areas that collect, store, or use PII will vary. It is imperative that the audit identify every department which uses PII—even if it is not gathered directly by that group—and include that department in the inventory and audit.

Employee PII and Privacy

Privacy audits should not only focus on external consumers, but must also deal with employee PII and the legal considerations impacting that data. Of particular interest will be the privacy of employee health information, which may be regulated by HIPAA. But other considerations must be taken into account. Much of the employee PII necessary for the data audit will reside within human resources and will often include information considered highly sensitive. You must determine exactly what information is collected and stored by HR, as well as the employees that have access to the information. Specifically, you will need to determine:

- What information is collected on employment applications?

- Are candidates' backgrounds checked?

- Is employee health information stored internally or managed by a third party?

- Who within the organization is responsible for maintenance and safeguarding of health benefit and life insurance information?

- Are claims for disability retained in a confidential, secure manner?

For each question listed above, you should determine how that information is collected, how the information is maintained, how the information is transmitted, with whom it is shared, who has access to the information, and how long the information is retained before deletion or destruction. Where information is handled by a third party, contracts should be assessed to ensure that they include provisions requiring that these parties' privacy and security provisions are equal to or exceed those of your organization.

As discussed previously, employee use of workplace communications tools has become a growing privacy concern on a number of levels. Employee monitoring occurs for a number of reasons, ranging from ensuring productivity to eliminating the risk of insecure transfer of confidential data or compromising network security. Employers must consider the legal ramifications of employee monitoring. For example, if the employer is planning

Making Sure Work Computers Are For Work

These days, it is not uncommon for businesses to have a policy that forbids the use of office electronic equipment for non–work-related purposes. The more clearly you send this message to employees, the better protected you should be if a problem develops.

Two recent criminal cases in which employees were discovered to have child pornography on their computers provide some lessons in effective computer use policies. In one case, the employer had not specifically informed employees that they could not store personal files on computers and that their Internet use would be monitored.[73] In the other case, the employer had conveyed this information to the employee through an extensive written policy and by way of a "splash page" that appeared on the computer screen every time the computer was turned on.[74] Not surprisingly, the court in the first case determined that the employee had greater privacy rights than the employee in the second case. Although both of these convictions were upheld, a prudent employer should provide clear use policies and set expectations to ensure they can maintain maximum control over business assets and rogue employees.

to monitor employee communications, he or she should be aware that the Electronic Communications Privacy Act allows monitoring of communications on company systems,[71] but that case law may not permit monitoring of personal calls without notice and consent. Courts have held that if an employer realizes that a call is personal, and not business related, the employer must cease monitoring the call.[75] Regardless, if the employer wishes to moni-

Blogs and PII: Your Employee's Diary Is Public

Theo Chance, a new IT employee, has a personal weblog (blog) where he writes about a variety of topics, including technology and "work stuff." His supervisor finds out that Theo has identified company employees by name on his blog and detailed their stupid exploits. He has mentioned security breaches and how IT mishandled the problem. When Theo's supervisor, Lu Lu Wong, confronts him about the weblog, Theo becomes indignant and tells Lu Lu that it's "personal," done on his time, and not related to the company. How could this problem have been prevented?

1. Theo's hyper-independence and attitude should have been uncovered by HR, so we need to bolster the interview process.
2. Company policy should make clear that all company information, including employees' names and email addresses, should not be used for non-business related activities.
3. Company policy should state that the company owns all company information, including personal information about its customers, clients, business partners, and employees, and employees are strictly prohibited from its use beyond work without the written authorization to do so by a manager.
4. The company should anticipate that employees will use information obtained at work for non-work purposes, and develop detailed rules to address situations like Theo's.

While clearly number 1 is not the best solution, numbers 2, 3 and 4 all have proactive partial solutions that could help address this kind of problem. Blog content is becoming a significant employer issue; more than 8 million Americans are blogging, and employees have been fired for putting company information on personal blogs.

tor employee communications, whether by telephone, email, instant messaging, or other channel, employee notice should be given and consent obtained. During the privacy audit, it is essential to ascertain:

- What notice, if any, is provided to employees regarding monitoring of workplace communications?

- Is written consent being obtained?

Auditing employee data will have unique features in the overall PII audit. Although the primary focus of the audit is consumer PII, employee privacy also involves risk management. Former employees may be litigious, and privacy is a ripe area for plaintiffs' attorneys. By including employee privacy as part of the overall PIM program, the organization may be taking important strides toward removing or mitigating a claim as part of employee lawsuits.

Data Flow Mapping

Once the data inventory has been completed, the auditors should map the flow of data inside and outside of the organization. The purpose of data flow mapping is to document the lifecycle of PII in order to ensure that every collection, use, transfer, and disposal of PII is done in accord with all applicable laws, industry standards, and relevant consumer demands. This is a non-technical process that typically involves interviewing department heads and other personnel that use or manage data. These interviews should be designed to uncover the actual data handling practices of the employees within each department.

The basic starting point for data flow mapping is to determine and record the points at which data is collected by a department. These collection points may include:

- A wide variety of online forms
- Email
- Call centers
- Customer loyalty programs
- Point of purchase
- Contests
- Surveys

- Warranty cards
- Order forms
- Chat rooms
- Marketing lists

The point-of-origin of PII is important, as it may affect the legal requirements that apply. This, in turn, will establish the baseline requirements for any policy regarding that data. For example, if email is a method your organization uses to collect PII, the CAN-SPAM Act should be taken into consideration when authoring policies and procedures. Or if PII is collected from the EU or Canada, the EU Data Protection Directive or PIPEDA, respectively, may apply. Point-of-origin is also important because it may help the auditors identify why the information was collected. As discussed earlier, data use should be limited to the purposes for which it was collected. Although this is not required under most domestic privacy laws (it *is* a standard fair information practice and is required under many international laws including the EU Data Protection Directive), it increasingly is a customer expectation.

Because the audit requires detailed information, department heads should be given ample time to prepare for the interview regarding their information needs and current practices. They should be prepared to discuss:

- Data collection
- Data maintenance and security
- Data use
- Disclosure of data to third parties
- Data deletion and/or destruction

Each of these areas requires careful questioning. With data collection, for example, the auditor will need to explore the following topics, among others:

- **After an individual volunteers information, does the organization gather further data to supplement the volunteered information?** If so, by what means is the supplemental information gathered? For example, is consumer PII such as name and address ever sent to a data management company to obtain overlay data, such as buying habits?

- **Once PII has been collected, is the data entry handled inhouse or is it outsourced?** If outsourced, what are the privacy practices of the third parties that handle this data? (Remember that some laws—like HIPAA—mandate the type of security used by the third party.)

- **Does any of the PII being collected come from outside the United States?** Does this bring it under any international privacy laws?

Review Existing Privacy Policies

The final step in the privacy audit is to gather and review all existing privacy polices and procedures. A thorough analysis should be conducted comparing the actual information handling practices found in each department with all documented policies and training materials. It is critical to review both departmental and enterprise-wide policies and procedures. As part of the audit you should check for any contradictory or confusing provisions in these policies. If gaps are found between the written policies and procedures and the actual practices found during the audit, steps should be taken immediately to fix them. These steps will likely take one of three basic paths:

- Revision of existing policies and procedures to reflect current PIM practices. (This may need to be done during an interim basis, to ensure compliance with existing policies while the new PIM strategy is developed.)

- Implementation of training and monitoring to ensure that PIM practices are changed immediately to match existing policies and procedures.

- Investment in technology to ensure PIM that is compliant with existing policies and all legal and regulatory restrictions.

No matter which steps are taken, follow-up audits of affected departments should be conducted to ensure that all gaps have in fact been closed.

Formulating a Privacy Policy

Formulating a Privacy Policy

13

An Effective Privacy Policy Is a Business Necessity

Robust privacy policies have become ubiquitous in the online world. The maze of online disclaimers and notices is a direct result of legislation and court judgments that protect PII. But a privacy policy must do more than simply the bare legal minimum. For better or worse, privacy is an emotional issue for consumers around the world. Many people feel as though there is a full frontal assault on their private information. They believe they have little or no control over the collection and use of their PII. As a result, a privacy policy must be designed to allay consumers' concerns and make them comfortable with doing business with your organization.

Consumers will expect you to have a privacy policy and they may have preconceptions about what it should say. A recent survey revealed that 57 percent of U.S. adults who use the Internet at home believe that when a website has a privacy policy, it will not share the PII they gather with other websites or businesses.[75] Consumers who believe an online merchant will deal with their PII in a manner consistent with their wishes are more likely to conduct business online. Businesses that take unfair advantage of that trust do so at their shareholders' peril.

As your PIM team begins to formulate its privacy policy, it must keep two goals in mind: the policy must reassure consumers and it must satisfy the legal and industry requirements. Remember that the provision of notice of your privacy practices should not be limited to your online visitors. If you collect, maintain, and use consumer PII, notice should be provided via the Internet, postal mail, and any others means to notify your customers about your organization's use of their PII.

Drafting privacy policies that comply with applicable laws, while addressing consumer sensitivities and reflecting business

No Notice? The Public Responds

In 2003, one of the nation's most recognized retailers settled a class-action suit brought by its credit card holders. The card owners claimed that the retailer violated California law when it shared customer information with third-party vendors without disclosing in its privacy policy that it would do so. The plaintiffs claimed that the retail giant received as much as 20 percent of the sales price of items that these third-party vendors marketed and sold to its card holders.

To settle the lawsuit, the retailer agreed to provide the plaintiffs with merchandise certificates and discounts worth more than $60 million. It also shelled out approximately $1.5 million in attorney fees and costs. In addition, it agreed to revise its privacy policy to inform customers that their information may be shared with third-party vendors and to give customers an opportunity to opt-out of this sharing.[76]

In an Effort to Comply, a Breach

In March 2005, the *Wall Street Journal* revealed that a number of mutual fund companies had posted their clients' names and account numbers on a publicly accessible website. The disclosure was apparently made pursuant to SEC regulations that require disclosure of the names of shareholders of more than 5 percent of a class of shares. The law did not require the account numbers, but the mutual fund companies apparently included them in the report because their database revealed that information when it calculated the shareholders who held the requisite amount. Needless to say, the shareholders were none too pleased to discover that their names and account numbers were available on the Web.[77]

objectives, is a tremendous challenge in and of itself. But the perpetually changing nature of business, the law, and the threats to digital data have made compliance with privacy policies even more difficult. Many organizations assume that once their policy is in place, the job is completed. This is a mistake. Every time content or services are added, or website functionality is changed, there is a risk of exposing users to privacy breaches and running afoul of the controlling laws. It is critical to every online business that as the business changes, the policy is reviewed to see if changes to meet the new challenges are necessary.

After your PIM team has completed its data audit, and the team has a good grasp on what data is currently being collected, the PIM team needs to consider the organization's goals—not only its compliance goals, but also its business goals. What information does the business need? What more could it use? Is it collecting more than necessary?

Determining Privacy Goals and Objectives

When the time comes to sit down and make determinations about your organization's privacy objectives, the process must serve two ends. As a matter of legal necessity, the organization must take steps to comply—and remain in compliance—with all state and federal laws regulating the manner in which PII is collected, maintained, and used within specific industries. These laws, such as GLBA, HIPAA, CAN-SPAM and COPPA, represent the floor—*the minimum necessary*—for an effective PIM program. For organizations doing business on a global basis, they must consider a multitude of international laws as well. For business purposes, the plan must determine the ceiling, or how high an organization can go, in developing privacy practices that will boost company performance and shareholder value. The team must recognize that the development of privacy policies and procedures creates an opportunity to gain consumer confidence. A higher degree of consumer trust will result in increased opt-in requests, better database maintenance, greater customer loyalty, and more detailed knowledge about consumers and customers. Handled poorly, privacy issues will cause potential customers to seek out competitors with better practices, subject your organization to the legal consequences and negative publicity of violations, and leave shareholders with declining portfolios.

One issue that is likely to come up is the sharing or sale of PII to third parties. It may be difficult to determine the value of these relationships. There is a strong consumer preference for limiting the use of their PII to the organization to which they volunteered it, as evidenced by numerous polls and surveys that found overwhelming support for keeping PII confidential. Economists and other business professionals, however, are often skeptical of such polls. Rather than accepting what consumers say, they prefer to look at what they do. This is known as consumers' "revealed preferences."[78] Several studies have demonstrated that consumers are willing to supply PII to companies online and offline if they are given some identifiable benefit in return.

These competing pictures of consumer preferences must inform the development of your organization's privacy policy. In deciding between a restrictive privacy policy or one that generally allows the sharing of PII, you will need to consider risk reduction strategies along with the pressure on the industry from consumer groups, state attorneys general, the plaintiffs' bar, and legislators.

Drafting Your Privacy Policies and Procedures

In setting down an organization's new practices, it is important to understand the difference between "policies" and "procedures." Policies provide a "high-level articulation of an organization's position on a particular issue," while "procedures bring those positions down to earth by laying out specific actions and responsibilities."[79] The procedures provide the detail and direction necessary for employees to effectively adhere to the policies.

In the case of a "privacy policy" that is intended for public distribution, the term is more than just an articulation of an organization's position. It is viewed by the public and by government agencies as creating an obligation to abide by the statements made within the privacy policy. It should be treated as "binding" between the organization and the consumer providing PII.

To get started on the development of policies and procedures, PIM team members responsible for each department or business division must carefully review the audit reports for their department. Among the questions they should answer about their area's use of PII are:

- Is there a legitimate business need for the collection and use of each type of PII being collected?

- From what countries did the PII originate or where is the information "owner" located?

- What legal restrictions may apply to the use of the type of PII being collected?

- What job functions within the department need to have access to the PII being collected and maintained?

- Are there security provisions at the departmental level to safeguard the PII and prevent it from being viewed by unauthorized parties?

- Will the PII be transferred to any other departments or divisions within the organization, and if so, for what purposes?

- Will the PII need to be transferred to any external third parties, and if so, for what purposes?

- How long will the department need to maintain the PII?

- How, when, and by whom will the PII be destroyed?

The answers to these questions will guide the development of privacy procedures for the department in question. This, in turn, will inform the drafting of policies and procedures for the entire enterprise. By reviewing the departmental audit reports, the team members get a structured look at the relevant privacy issues. This leads not only to a vision of the privacy policy, but it may also reveal new ways in which data can be managed. For example, by seeing which employees have access to PII, a manager may conceive of how to limit unnecessary access to PII, thereby improving data security. Likewise, a review of the audit report of a department's data retention practices may reveal that gigabytes of data can be purged, because it is no longer needed and has met its retention period for record keeping purposes. Perhaps the audits will reveal that some of the data being collected isn't being used at all and the collection can cease.

Armed with the critical information revealed by the audit reports, the team will be well prepared to develop the policies that will guide the organization's PIM initiative, along with the procedures through which the program will be implemented. The team will recognize that there are legal and business requirements that must be met, depending on the type of PII in question. Departmental policies must address a wide range of issues, from HR's handing of employee health information to the marketing department's activities that may be governed by federal laws such as Gramm-Leach-Bliley or CAN-SPAM. The legal team should be enlisted to help determine which laws are applicable, and what must be done to meet the requirements.

Once the team is confident in the "hard" requirements—legal and regulatory restrictions, as well as risk management necessities—the PIM team can consider just how consumer friendly the organization's privacy policies and practices can be. Again, while this may seem a secondary reason for undertaking a privacy management project, privacy is an opportunity to increase shareholder value. Remember, when considering the value of a publicly disclosed privacy policy, transparency is key. A clearly written and easily understood policy leads to greater consumer trust and bottom-line benefits.

When drafting your public privacy policy, you should carefully consider each of the foundational elements of privacy discussed in part one of this book:

- **Notice**—What will you tell consumers and employees? How will you tell them? What if they have questions? How can they learn more?

- **Choice**—Will consumers be given the choice to opt-in to sharing of data? Or will they have to opt-out? How will they make their election?

- **Access**—Who will have access to the data? Will your customers understand exactly who will have their data and what it will be used for? What about internal information? Who has access to employee health data? How could it end up in the wrong hands and what can be done now to prevent that from happening?

- **Third-party transfer**—What relationships exist that require the sharing of information? How much income is generated

Clarity and Simplicity of Privacy Policy Language Could be the Difference Between Winning and Losing

Which language would be easier for the average employee to understand?

1. Every employee and any and all third parties working for the company, or on its behalf, or in a facility owned by the company or an affiliated company, shall use all reasonable means to seek to protect the information our customers expect to be adequately protected.

2. All employees must protect personal information of our customers and other employees. Please consult the IT Information Security Classification Policy if you need help determining what security measures need to be taken to protect such information or what information constitutes personal information.

3. Please make sure you properly secure personal information (which includes Social Security number, name, address, driver's license number, bank account information, etc.) of our customers and employees.

   a. Personal information must never be sent via email unless it is encrypted. (The encryption technology is available from the information security department).
   b. Personal information must never be sent via fax unless you do a test transmission of the number confirming it is the correct recipient and then hit redial to ensure it is going to the correct number.
   c. Don't leave personal information on your desk.
   d. Make sure you close all documents containing personal information on your desktop before you leave your computer.

4. Properly secure all personal information.

The best answer is (3), because it is the clearest and provides specific rules to secure information when using different office tools. Number (2) has good aspects, but it is probably unrealistic to expect employees to stop and look up a separate policy to figure out the applicable rules and procedures. Number (1) is too lawyerly and leaves too much to employees to interpret. Number (4) is too vague. Remember the best policies and company directives are clear, straightforward, and as short as possible.

from sale of PII to third parties? How much revenue would be lost from consumers who don't want their information shared? What are the policies and practices of your competitors? What is the likelihood that your own business may want to start sharing more data in the future?

- **Security**—Where is the information stored and is it sufficiently secure? How is the information transmitted or transferred and is it a secure method? Who has access to the data? How carefully have you screened these employees? How old are your security systems? Who is responsible for updating the technology? How often is it updated?

- **Enforcement**—How will you know when the policy has been violated? Will violators be disciplined? Who will handle customer complaints? How will the company respond to a breach?

Weigh each of these elements as they relate to the goals and objectives of your PIM program. This will help you draft the language for each element in your publicly disclosed privacy policy.

Making Your Policies Known to the Public

Your organization's privacy policy must be communicated in clear terms to the public at large. This policy must explain the actual data handling practices of the enterprise. These practices should meet applicable legal standards and serve the information needs of the business. In the past, public dissemination of a company's privacy policy was generally considered a good business decision and, for online businesses, a demonstration that the organization was an ethical online citizen. It was a practice that reassured a distrustful public of an organization's commitment to responsible business practices. Today, a posted privacy policy is sometimes a legal requirement (e.g., for any online organization collecting PII on a resident of California.)[80] Recall that the California Online Privacy Protection Act requires a conspicuously displayed privacy policy that discloses:

- The categories of information being collected

- The categories of third parties with which the information may be shared

- A description of any mechanism by which a consumer can access his or her PII

- A description of the manner by which a consumer will be notified of any changes to the privacy policy

Remember: Tone and Transparency

Privacy policies should not be filled with legal jargon or confusing terms. Nor should a privacy policy be written to intentionally confuse or dupe a reader into sharing his or her PII. Your policy's language should cater to your customers' concerns about privacy and reluctance to share confidential information.

It is critical that the PIM team identify your organization's customers and potential customers when it begins to write these policies. If your organization is a bricks-and-mortar retailer, you may have seen studies and survey results showing that customers generally do not mind sharing PII. Your privacy policies should be written in a manner which reflects this existing comfort level. On the other hand, if you are part of a highly-regulated financial services company, for which there may be a relatively low degree of consumer trust, your privacy policies must be written to clearly and thoroughly explain the institution's information handling practices. Your policy should try to make customers feel comfortable sharing their PII with you. Even when the legal requirements are complex, as they are for online businesses, you must formulate a policy that is as clear and comprehensible as possible.

Take a look at the different tone of two privacy policies. First, consider the policy of a nationally recognized retailer:

Welcome to _____ (www._____.com). We fully under-stand that your trust is our most important asset. We take the protection and proper use of your personal information seriously and are committed to protecting your personal information in our possession. In order to preserve your trust, we want you to understand what personally identifiable or personal information we may collect from you when you visit our website, how we use such information, and the choices you have regarding our use of this information.

Now consider the language of a nationally recognized financial services company:

This Privacy Policy explains what _____ does to keep information about you private and secure. We want you to know how we manage that information to serve you and that you have choices about how it is shared.

Q. Who is Covered by the Privacy Policy?

A. This Privacy Policy covers the _____ family of compa-nies. The following is a partial list of the U.S. consumer financial services companies owned by _____:

. . .

This Policy applies to our current and former consumer customers. Separate policies may apply to customers of certain businesses, such as Private Banking. Also, customers in certain states will get policies that apply to them. The privacy policies posted on our websites apply when you use those sites. In addition, you can view _____ Online Consumer Information Practices.

Notice how the first privacy policy—the one from the national retailer—takes the time and space to set the consumer at ease using terms like "trust," "protection," and "choice." The financial services company, on the other hand, quickly gets into the substance of the policy. It does not start out with a consumer friendly tone. Rather, it is a bit more confusing from the start, as it attempts to explain to whom the policy applies and how it may differ for individuals in different states. While the privacy policy in the financial services example was likely drafted with legal compliance in mind, the language of the retail policy goes a long way toward building consumer trust and reducing the risks. This effort to placate the consumer leads to measurable benefits.

Regardless of whether an organization conducts business online or offline (or both), well-developed privacy policies and procedures serve another important function—they can help an organization mitigate any damages in the event of a lawsuit or FTC investigation. Many privacy laws impose greater penalties for willful violations. These penalties may include prison sentences. Well-documented policies, procedures, training programs, and monitoring systems dramatically reduce the possibility of such penalties. With documented safeguards in place, any privacy violations that do occur are more likely to be viewed by the courts or the FTC as isolated mistakes, not enterprise-wide privacy failures. A well-formulated and implemented PIM plan is evidence that business executives were committed to proper data management. Such evidence may be valuable in an era of increased shareholder scrutiny and greater corporate accountability.

While the Law Plays Catch-Up, Technology May Help

ID theft, pharming, and phishing scams have hit the financial services community hard. While politicians wrangle with a legislative response, some financial institutions are undertaking voluntary steps to increase customer confidence. Some financial services companies are issuing customer IDs and passwords, plus a special security technology "token" that provides an additional layer of authentication for online transactions. When these customers do business online, they have two forms of ID and more comfort that they won't be the next one scammed.

Internal Privacy Policies and Procedures

So far, we have described the formulation of publicly-facing privacy policies—the policy distributed to customers and made available on your organization's website. But what about the policy that governs your inhouse management of data, including your own employees' PII? Your PIM team should be every bit as concerned with this policy as it is with the external PIM policy.

Internal privacy policies and procedures should state, for the benefit of every individual within your organization, exactly what your personal information management policies are, and precisely what steps each employee must take to ensure that those policies are met. These documents dictate the collection, maintenance, and use of PII within your organization. They set out specific rules that must be followed for different categories of PII to which different legal restrictions apply. For example, there may be significant differences between the policy you decide should govern collection and use of employee PII as opposed to a policy that would govern client PII.

As is the case with your public policies, your internal policy and procedures must be clearly written. Employees need to understand what is expected of them, the reasons behind the expectations, and the consequences if they fail to meet their obligations. Without effective and comprehensible internal policies and procedures, employees are bound to make information management mistakes.

Your internal privacy policies and procedures will continue beyond the tenure of individual managers and supervisors who oversee departmental PIM procedures. By creating a written policy and set of procedures, your PIM team will generate a memory

Know the Threat

Which poses a greater threat to information security today: employees or people and groups outside the organization? According to a recent *Wall Street Journal* article, in 2004, 50 percent of all security problems came from inside the company. That was an increase from 30 percent the year before.[81]

bank for the organization. It also will ease transitions in and out of your organization, as the company's approach to privacy will not be tied to an individual's management approach.

To ensure that your internal privacy policies and procedures are read and understood by all employees, they should be referenced, summarized, or included in your employee handbooks. The privacy policy for the organization should be mandatory reading for each new hire. Documentation in handbooks should include examples and illustrations. They should be broken down into easily digestible sections so that they are clearly understood.

For positions that deal directly with PII or other confidential information, employees should be required to read, in their entirety, all policies that apply to the information they will be handling. It may be advisable to require each new employee to sign an acknowledgement that he or she understands the importance of privacy to the welfare of the organization and will adhere to all privacy policies

You Make the Call

ABC Insurance Company wants to build a relationship with the entire family to ensure it does business into the future with existing customers and their children. The marketing staff develops a campaign for a new company website, Financial Fun for Kids. One of the prizes the website plans to give away to "young investors" who visit the site is a blowup pool cartoon character. You are on the committee overseeing this venture. Do you have any concerns?

You should. Remember that the Children's Online Privacy Protection Act (COPPA) covers situations like this one, where a company creates a commercial website that is targeting children under 13. Given that most pool toys will be played with by kids in the protected age group, COPPA is likely to apply. ABC must be careful about the PII it collects from kids and needs to provide parents with sufficient notice about the company's information gathering practices, as well as get parental consent prior to any collection, use, or disclosure of the PII. Parents must also have the right to review the information collected and refuse to allow the company to use it. Finally, the company should make sure that the pool toy is not given conditioned upon the child disclosing PII.

and procedures. The acknowledgement should clearly state the consequences for failure to follow privacy policies and procedures and should be a mandatory inclusion in each employee's personnel file.

For Example: The Better Business Bureau Sample Privacy Policy: Externally Facing

Effective month/day/year

Our Commitment to Privacy

Your privacy is important to us. To better protect your privacy we provide this notice explaining our online information practices and the choices you can make about the way your information is collected and used.

The Information We Collect

This notice applies to all information collected or submitted on the XYZ company website. On some pages, you can order products, make requests, and register to receive materials. The types of personal information collected at these pages, may include:

- Name
- Address
- Email address
- Phone number
- Credit/Debit card information

On some pages, you can submit information about other people. For example, if you order a gift online and want it sent directly to the recipient, you will need to submit the recipient's address. In this circumstance, the types of personal information collected are:

- Name
- Address
- Phone Number

How We Use Information

We use the information you provide about yourself when placing an order only to complete that order. We do not share this information with outside parties except to the extent necessary to complete that order.

We use the information you provide about someone else when placing an order only to ship the product and to confirm delivery. We do not share this information with outside parties except to the extent necessary to complete that order.

We use return email addresses to answer the email we receive. Such addresses are not used for any other purpose and are not shared with outside parties.

You can register on our website if you would like to receive our catalog and updates on new products and services. Information you submit on our website will not be used for this purpose unless you fill out the registration form.

We use non-identifying and aggregate information to better design our website and to share with advertisers. For example, we may tell an advertiser that X number of individuals visited a certain area on our website, or that Y number of men and Z number of women filled out our registration form, but we would not disclose anything that could be used to identify those individuals.

Finally, we never use or share the personally identifiable information provided to us online in ways unrelated to the ones described above without also providing an opportunity to opt-out or otherwise prohibit such unrelated uses.

Our Commitment to Data Security

To prevent unauthorized access, maintain data accuracy, and ensure the correct use of information, we have put in place appropriate physical, electronic, and administrative procedures to safeguard and secure the information we collect online.

Our Commitment to Children's Privacy

Protecting the privacy of the very young is especially important. For that reason, we never collect or maintain information at our website from those we actually know are under 13, and no part of our website is structured to attract anyone under 13.

How You Can Access or Correct Your Information

You can access all your personally identifiable information that we collect online and maintain by [description of the company access procedure]. We use this procedure to better safeguard your information. You can correct factual errors in your personally identifiable information by sending us a request that credibly shows the error.

To protect your privacy and security, we take reasonable steps to verify your identity before granting access or making corrections.

How to Contact Us

Should you have questions or concerns about these policies, please call us at _____ or send us an email at _____.[82]

Implementing the Policy 14

With a policy in hand, you are ready to get it in place and get on with business. Not so fast. Implementing an effective PIM strategy requires more than just printing up the policy and dropping it off on your employees' desks. In fact, before you take any affirmative steps to implement the policy, you must start by ensuring that your policy will achieve the organization's PIM goals. The first step for implementation, then, is a gap analysis.

Conducting a Gap Analysis

The gap analysis is a careful comparison of your existing PIM practices against your new PIM policies and procedures. The gap analysis is not intended to cause you to rewrite or challenge your new policy. Rather it is to ensure that existing practices in need of updating are unearthed and addressed as part of the implementation. Like the privacy audit, it must be conducted by qualified internal resources, or by third party privacy professionals. This side-by-side comparison of the current privacy practices with the new PIM structure will expose any gaps that need to be filled before you can put the new policies and procedures to work.

If you find gaps, remedial steps must be taken before you implement your PIM program. During the analysis, you will discover a variety of ways that gaps may be addressed. These patches often require a broad array of internal and external resources. For example, in order to fill a gap, it may be necessary to retrain specific employees in select jobs or you may need to move certain paper records to more secure locations or implement new procedures for destruction of PII. Or you may find that your new PIM program requires the installation of new enterprise-wide security software. Remember that when these gaps are found, it may not always be in the interest of the organization to change the existing procedure. Existing practices may satisfy the privacy principals for which the organization is striving. If that is the case, minor adjustments may be made to specific, limited portions of the new PIM program.

In addition to identifying the adjustments that will need to be made as your organization transitions to its new PIM processes, the gap analysis also serves as another opportunity for any refinements to the new policies and procedures. Because the gap analysis requires close, focused attention on the new policies, the process may expose ambiguities or conflicts that exist between, for example, enterprise-wide policies and procedures and those that exist on a departmental level only. The analysis may also expose gaps between the new policies and procedures and legal requirements impacting certain business units. These discrepancies are best resolved through the gap analysis process. The failure to do so may create inconsistent PIM practices that can reduce the effectiveness of the PIM program, or require retraining and re-implementation of practices. Better to scrutinize the new PIM procedures carefully before they are implemented.

As part of the gap analysis, the PIM team should evaluate whether the policies and procedures achieve the organization's overall goals. This aspect of the gap analysis goes beyond the legal considerations and business objectives that were the focus of the policy and procedure development stage. It looks for gaps between the newly developed PIM procedures and privacy management "best practices." Specific areas that might be considered during this phase of the gap analysis include:

- Whether any new roles and responsibilities will be created, such as chief privacy officer

- Whether new outside services will be used, such as legislative tracking services

- Whether new training and job aids will be added in addition to those identified as PIM necessities

- Whether new employee recognition or reward programs will be implemented

Decisions on these issues may require input from the executive level. Many of the items in question go beyond the scope of PIM necessities and they may require additional budgetary allocations.

Identify PII Vulnerabilities

In the process of conducting the gap analysis, the audit team should identify vulnerabilities in the security of PII maintained by your organization and being transferred to third parties. When explicit promises are made about the security of PII, companies may be legally obligated to take reasonable steps to guard against foreseeable vulnerabilities. These vulnerabilities often reside in the space between the newly developed PIM procedures and the existing practices. For example, new policies may require that no PII be stored on the hard drive of employees with direct Internet access from their desktop computers. However, the elimination of this vulnerability requires more than simply issuing the new policy and hoping that employees comply. It requires an up-front effort and hands-on examination of workplace computers to ensure elimination of the vulnerability. Other vulnerabilities to watch for during the gap analysis may include:

- Out-of-date virus protection programs

- New technologies or products being used by your organization that do not meet the standards set forth in the PIM initiative

- Overlooked security alerts or updates provided by software manufacturers

- Inadequate password protection or other user authentication processes

- Lack of a system to identify attempted unauthorized access to PII or other potential security breaches

- Lack of an incident recovery or back-up plan in the event of a security breach

- Inadequate review and testing of your security systems

The vulnerabilities you may discover during the gap analysis may not be limited to technological issues. The analysis should also take into account the manner in which employees use PII and how that use may compromise data security and integrity. For example, your new policies will likely limit access to PII to certain job functions. Your actual practices must reflect this, typically via the immediate implementation of monitoring of employee access to and use of PII.

Uncover Those Vulnerabilities or the FTC Will

Even large companies that prioritize information security can drop the ball. One company that created a service through which Web surfers could negotiate most of their online transactions promised its users that it would keep their information secure. The information at issue included financial information such as credit card numbers. In 2002, the FTC filed a complaint alleging that there were significant security problems within the program that could jeopardize the privacy of millions of consumers. The complaint alleged that the company did not employ "sufficient measures reasonable and appropriate under the circumstances to maintain and protect the privacy and confidentiality" of PII. The complaint also alleged that the company failed to implement systems that would prevent or detect unauthorized access or monitor for potential vulnerabilities.

The final FTC order in the case prohibited any misrepresentations about the use of, and protection for, PII and required the company to implement a comprehensive information security program. The company also was required to have an independent professional certify, every two years, that the company's information security program met or exceeded the standards in the order and continues to operate effectively.[84]

The importance of the gap analysis cannot be overstated. It is your last, best chance to prevent "kinks" in the system once your PIM plan is deployed. The failure to spot problems and address them could cost your organization time, money, and credibility with regulators and customers.

Gaps in Third Party Contracts

A critical element of your gap analysis, and one that is sometimes overlooked, is a review of your contracts with third party vendors. The aim of this review is to ensure that all contracts that address the transfer of PII to or the use of PII by a third party meet the standards of your new PIM policies. For example, all contracts which address the conveyance of PII to a third party should now include contract language that reflects the directives contained in the new policy. The contract should also prescribe the acceptable procedures for maintenance and security of PII while in possession of the third party, as well as acceptable methods for the destruction or return of the PII upon completion of the job. Each contract must be reviewed, and, if necessary, amended to meet the standards of your PIM practices. Because of the technical nature of this review, and the possible need to draft legally binding documents, your corporate counsel or legal department should be involved in this process.

Keep in mind that reviewing third party contracts for compliance is not just a question of best practices; it may be the law. For example, the HIPAA Privacy Rule includes stringent requirements regarding business associate agreements. Specifically, a contract between an entity subject to HIPAA and a business associate must provide (in part) that the business associate will:

- not use or further disclose the information other than as permitted or required by the contract or as required by law;

- use appropriate safeguards to prevent use or disclosure of the information other than as provided for by its contract;

- report to the covered entity any use or disclosure of the information not provided for by its contract of which it becomes aware; and

- ensure that any agents, including a subcontractor, to whom it provides protected health information received from, or created or received by the business associate on behalf of, the covered entity agrees to the same restrictions and conditions that apply to the business associate with respect to such information.[85]

Your gap analysis will identify the associates and vendors with which your organization will need to agree on the adequate level of privacy protection for the information being shared.

Implementing the New Privacy Practices, Procedures, and Policies

With a thorough gap analysis completed, the PIM team is ready to implement the new PIM scheme. The implementation stage requires a substantial level of change throughout your organization. As business executives should know by now, employees are often reluctant or resistant to change. This is particularly true if the changes are as broad and serious as those that will be required during and after the implementation of the PIM program. Some of the PIM elements that will likely meet resistance include:

- Restrictions on data flow such as newly required user authentication and/or passwords in order to access certain data

- The restriction of information flow into certain departments within the organization

- Putting physical safeguards in place: door locks, file cabinet locks, even positioning computer monitors so that PII cannot be viewed by unauthorized parties

- The presence of new technological data security systems designed to prevent unauthorized internal and external access to confidential information

Of course, the reasons for these changes should be explained to the workforce. Your organization should distribute documentation explaining the pertinent elements of the PIM program and new PII-handling rules. Your PIM team should have a plan to train and educate the workforce about the new PIM strategy. Employees need to understand the reasons for the program and the consequences of privacy failures and breaches.

As discussed in chapter 11, enterprise-wide buy-in is essential to the effective implementation and continued success of your new PIM practices. But perhaps the term "buy-in" does not truly convey the goal here. The ultimate goal is the creation of an atmosphere of urgency so that employees pay attention to the new PIM program.

As we have stated earlier in this book, privacy is an issue—a 21st century business imperative—that flows from the top of the organization down. This is especially so because managers may view privacy protection as a cost center, instead of a profitable practice. Company executives must emphasize the benefits of PIM and its priority. There are a number of steps that should be taken, at both the executive and department-head level, that will encourage employees to buy-in to PIM during and after the implementation stage.

Effective communication is vital. Your team must carefully consider the messages it wants to communicate, and how those messages can be effectively delivered. Even the timing of the communication should be carefully planned to achieve maximum impact and not become routine and in danger of being overlooked or ignored. We've addressed many of the tactics for communicating privacy throughout the organization earlier in the book: CEO presentations about privacy to the entire organization, executive-level memos detailing the importance of privacy, presentations made available via an Intranet, and so on. Thought should also be given to delivering specific messages that are tailored to departments and the types of PII they handle, along with the risks presented by that information.

All of these tools should be used to construct a solid business case for privacy, one that will be understood and carry weight with all employees, regardless of their seniority. The business case will focus on the two sides of the privacy coin—risk management and bottom line benefit to the organization. The critical nature of the PIM program should be stressed, with examples of benefits to organizations that have handled privacy correctly and detriments to those that have fallen victim to careless or inadequate privacy practices.

Communications should also identify one or two examples of how responsible and legally compliant PIM practices have already benefited the organization, as well as other businesses. Such examples will generate positive support among employees and encourage compliance with the new PIM processes. This tactic should continue throughout the life of the PIM program. Sharing positive results and publicizing employee compliance will build momentum of the PIM program.

Develop a PIM Implementation "Roadmap"

To further accommodate the changes in PIM, an implementation roadmap should be developed for each department that handles PII. These roadmaps, to be prepared by the department head (who may be a member of the PIM team), must clearly describe how the new PIM system will be implemented and what employees must do to make it successful. The map is essentially a guide from point A (where privacy practices sit at present) to point B (what the PIM program and privacy process will look like when implementation is complete).

Although there is no way for the roadmap to identify all of the issues and challenges that might arise along the way, reasonably foreseeable challenges should be anticipated and identified. If time and resources permit, solutions to these problems should be developed and provided to departmental staff prior to the implementation process. Departmental PIM roadmaps should not, however, be designed to solve every implementation problem. The actual processes will require contributions from those employees with the expertise necessary to achieve the end result. An example helps to clarify. Let's say that the roadmap indicates that currently, at point A, there is no security requirement within the HR department by which only authorized HR staff can access employee health-related information. The roadmap may indicate that this is a requirement at point B. It will be up to the HR department manager, likely in conjunction with IT, to develop a system by which such information is password protected. The roadmap will only indicate points A and B. It is up to the departments and the responsible individuals to reach the established PIM standard of point B.

Implementing Technological PIM Elements

Unlike other components of the PIM plan, the technological aspects of information management cannot be implemented by departmental personnel alone. These components fall under the purview of the IT department, which will need to address aspects of the PIM program implementation on both an enterprise-wide and departmental basis.

For IT personnel, the initial and one of the most critical elements of PIM implementation is the safeguarding of PII from unauthorized external access. Electronic PII must be stored on a secure server that is either inaccessible from the outside, or is only accessible externally via processes with strong security protections. Confidence in the security solutions is imperative. These solutions must be carefully researched, not only in terms of overall effectiveness and usability, but also for compatibility with your existing systems. Appropriate resources must be made available for the acquisition of security solutions. IT will need the full inventory of the PII collected by every department within the organization. IT also will want to employ safeguards that will secure backup media and archived data, in addition to the data that is being actively used. IT should be prepared to acquire, install, and activate any encryption technology that the organization will use to safeguard electronic data while it is stored on—or during transfer from—the organization's own servers. IT should also be prepared to take steps to limit or otherwise safeguard information stored on laptop computers. Your PIM program should include strict written policies regarding the use of laptops or other portable computers of any kind, and this information should be in the hands of all employees entrusted with the use of a laptop computer. Finally, IT must take steps to secure information stored on the hard drives of computers with Internet access. While hackers or other individuals seeking access to your organization's PII are likely to focus on the main servers, individual computers within your network can still be exploited as a gateway into your system. Every computer with a direct Internet connection must be protected from external attack.

Conduct Mandatory Privacy Training Workshops

Even after IT installs data privacy protections, mistakes happen. Just as a chain is only as strong as its weakest link, even the best PIM practices can be undone by the careless actions of a single employee. That is why ongoing employee education and monitoring is an essential element of your PIM initiatives. One of the most effective tools for communicating the importance of privacy to your employees is mandatory enterprise-wide privacy training workshops. Depending on the extent to which your employees handle PII, these may be held on a semiannual, annual, or biannual basis. The goal of the workshops—which should be conducted by designated privacy staff or a professional privacy trainer—is not only to teach employees the provisions of the PIM program itself, but also educate them about reasons behind the organizational focus on privacy. Employees often hear the dire warnings about the damage that occurs when PII is compromised. They should also know the benefits in revenue and customer acquisition and retention for organizations with an effective PIM program.

Training sessions should be crafted to educate or refresh participants in all foundational elements of privacy (notice, choice, access, third-party transfer, security, and enforcement) and how each element must be handled within the structure of the overall PIM program. Workshops also provide a necessary opportunity to remind employees of their personal responsibilities with regard to PII and possible consequences—to the organization as a whole and to each employee individually—of their failures.

Privacy training sessions provide the perfect opportunity to update staff on new privacy laws, changes to existing laws, and any resulting changes to policies. This is a critical function of training. Privacy law continues to develop at a rapid pace. Changes in data privacy laws will likely have immediate impact on PIM processes. Although the legal department will generally be aware of changes to privacy law, the rapid proliferation of these laws may leave them little time to brief all employees on each new provision. Department heads can serve as a critical conduit of information, passing on news of changes in privacy laws to the legal personnel and their own division's employees.

Like enterprise-wide privacy trainings, departmental training must occur. The departmental training sessions should focus on the types of data collected and used by department employees, any changes in legal requirements for managing that data, and any coinciding changes to the PIM criteria impacting their specific business unit. Departmental-level training should be held periodically, with sessions scheduled as necessary to keep all employees abreast of current developments.

Create a Privacy Resource Website

Another excellent way to spread the word about your new PIM program is a company-wide privacy resource website. This gives employees the opportunity to get up to speed on privacy during periods in which no training or workshops are taking place.

It also provides an optional way for employees to continue their privacy education at their own pace. Clearly, the more educated your employees become, the less risk there is of a privacy problem. Content of a privacy website might include some of the following, at a minimum:

- Your publicly facing privacy policy

- Internal privacy policies, including any departmental policies

- Written procedures or guidelines

- Additional materials explaining the importance of the PIM program

- A list of the foundational elements of privacy and explanations of each

- The manner in which privacy impacts your organization

- Consumer privacy concerns specific to your organization

- A quick reference guide for addressing consumer questions and concerns

Such a website might also include tutorials on the basics of privacy, along with self-assessment tools and tests. Some organizations have compiled extensive privacy resources, whereby employees can find a wealth of privacy information and develop a comprehensive understanding of privacy. Regardless of the size and scope of your privacy website, employees should be made aware that this resource is available at any time and its use should be encouraged.

Be Sure Employees In Customer Facing Positions Have Solid Privacy Training

Still not sure ongoing training and investment in education is worthwhile? Consider the actions of a customer service representative at a lingerie retailer call center. She received a call from a Web-savvy individual informing her that he was able to access, on the retailer's website, information about customers' recent purchases along with the customers' names, addresses, and other PII. The call center rep asked the caller whether he was able to access credit card information. When the caller replied that he was not, the customer service rep told him that it was not a problem in that case, and thanked him for calling.

Unfortunately for the lingerie retailer, its privacy policy stated that: "any information you provide to us at this site when you establish or update an account, enter a contest, shop online or request information...is maintained in private files on our secure Web server and internal systems..." And even more unfortunately for the retailer, the caller wasn't satisfied with the way this had been handled to date, so he contacted the press to let the public know what had happened. This, in turn, caught the attention of the New York Attorney General. The result for the lingerie retailer was a settlement decree, the terms of which required the company to:

- Establish and maintain an information security program to protect personal information
- Establish management oversight and employee training programs
- Hire an external auditor to annually monitor compliance with the security program
- Provide refunds or credits to all affected New York consumers
- Pay $50,000 to the State of New York for costs and penalties

Monitoring Compliance with the PIM Program

15

With the PIM program and training in place, the organization must now turn its attention to monitoring for adherence to the new privacy policies and procedures. The monitoring will occur on two levels: employee monitoring and systems monitoring. This will allow the organization to continually assess whether its PIM program is succeeding, and if not, to identify those places where it needs fixing. It will also arm the organization with information necessary to take corrective actions. In short, ongoing monitoring would allow the organization to uncover PIM problems before a consumer or watchdog group finds them and reports your organization to the FTC or the state attorney general's office, or files a private lawsuit. In the event of an investigation or legal action, a record of continuous monitoring demonstrates that the PIM program was more than just window dressing—it was in fact monitored and corrective actions taken when circumstances necessitated such.

Systems Monitoring

Your monitoring program should allow the IT administrators and other appropriate personnel to continually assess what PII-related activity is transpiring on the organization's networks. For several years now, newspapers have been filled with headlines about security breaches and unauthorized access to PII. Some recent laws, including California SB 1386, have effectively made monitoring of networks a requirement, as any breaches or exposure of consumer PII must be reported to consumers. Another area that deserves attention is employee authentication and use of passwords. Guidelines should be set for the creation and management of passwords. Employees should also be required to periodically change their passwords. The selection of passwords must be monitored to ensure that employees are not using easily guessable passwords that would make a network vulnerable to security breaches from internal or external threats.

Beefing Up Bank Security

The Federal Deposit Insurance Corporation has recommended that banks consider using modern password technology, employ software that detects suspicious activity, and increase consumer awareness of identity theft and its causes. The FDIC's recommendations were given in response to reports that nearly 2 million Americans had unauthorized transfers from their checking accounts in a 12-month period between 2003 and 2004. The FDIC found that identity theft has migrated from a problem for big banks to a problem for all banks, including small institutions.

Among the specific recommendations to increase security was a two-factor authorization system. In addition to entering a username and a password, the customer would provide a "code word" that would then be incorporated into any further communication between the bank and its customer. The FDIC also suggested banks flag large transactions and payments, excessive transactions, or the copying of fields from the bank's webpage.[87]

The FDIC has more than an oversight interest in cracking down on identity theft. In June of 2005, the FDIC disclosed that PII of more than 6,000 former and current FDIC employees was stolen. Some of the missing data—which included names, dates of birth, Social Security Numbers, and salary information—was used for fraudulent purposes. It is worth noting that reports attribute the theft not to an electronic breach, but to the theft of a paper document containing the relevant information.[88]

The Value of a Password

The FTC penalized a retailer for not properly securing PII that was subsequently stolen. The FTC determined that inadequate security alone, regardless of fault, was enough to determine the company violated regulations. The FTC determined that the company failed to encrypt consumer information and that other sensitive files were protected by commonly known default passwords.[89]

Employee Monitoring

By monitoring employee compliance—with full employee awareness of the monitoring activity—an organization can deter employees' variance from the policies and procedures with which they must comply. Of course, when it comes to public perception, an organization wants to continually demonstrate its commitment to excellent privacy practices. A practice of monitoring for compliance demonstrates to the outside world that the organization is truly committed to privacy and its PIM program.

Employee monitoring is mandatory in some instances. For example, the National Association of Securities Dealers (NASD), which, along with the SEC and other agencies regulates the securities industry, promulgates "Conduct Rules" with which its members must comply. One of these rules, Conduct Rule 3010, requires that NASD members "establish and maintain a system to supervise the activities of employees that is reasonably designed to achieve compliance with applicable securities laws and regulations."

Follow Your Privacy Policies

Compliance with your PIM program must be viewed on an organizational basis, as well as an individual basis. The importance of following your privacy policies cannot be overstated. Failure to adhere to privacy policies has been a common thread in FTC actions, personal lawsuits, and class actions, as well as actions by state attorneys general. The FTC has been particularly aggressive in pursuing businesses that have failed to comply with their privacy policies. The FTC's authority in this regard, in part, arises from Section 5 of the FTC Act, which prohibits unfair or deceptive practices.[90] Section 5 provides, in a pertinent part that:

> *Unfair methods of competition in or affecting commerce, and unfair or deceptive acts or practices in or affecting commerce, are hereby declared unlawful.*[91]

The FTC likely considers actions that are contrary to a company's privacy policies to fall within the scope of Section 5. The Commission has garnered numerous settlements against nationally and internationally known businesses, and it continues to actively investigate and file actions against businesses which it believes have failed to act in accord with their privacy policies.

Acting Outside of a Privacy Policy: The FTC Steps In

In April of 2004, a large U.S. music retailer agreed to settle FTC charges that a security flaw in its website exposed customers' PII to other Internet users, in violation of its privacy policy and federal law.

The music retailer's online privacy policy made claims such as "[w]e use state-of-the-art technology to safeguard your personal information," and "[y]our account information is password-protected. You and only you have access to this information." When the music retailer redesigned its site, however, a security vulnerability was created that allowed Web users to access the company's records and view certain PII about customers—including names, billing and shipping addresses, email addresses, phone numbers, and past purchases. The FTC claimed that the security flaw was easy to prevent and fix, but that the company failed to:

- implement appropriate checks and controls in the process of writing and revising its Web applications,
- adopt and implement policies and procedures to test the security of its website, and
- provide appropriate training and oversight for its employees.

The Commission charged that the music retailer's privacy policy assurances were therefore false and violated Section 5 of the FTC Act. The settlement agreement barred the company from future misrepresentations, required them to implement an appropriate security program, and to undergo website security audits by a qualified third-party security professional for ten years.[92]

As the case above demonstrates, it is not only intentional violations of privacy policies which draw the ire of consumers and the attention of the FTC. Your organization need not have intended to violate or have blatantly disregarded the privacy policy in order for the FTC to step in, conduct an investigation, and file charges. In this environment, privacy policy compliance is a vital risk management factor. This must be made crystal clear to all staff that may come into contact with PII.

The case of the music retailer also illustrates the fact that an organization must take extreme care when it changes its PIM practices. Any changes on the departmental or enterprise-wide level must be scrutinized by appropriate personnel—whether that be a chief privacy officer, the legal department, a manager responsible for departmental PIM, or a third party expert. The analysis will first focus on the necessity and scope of the changes and whether the changes are the minimum necessary to meet objectives. The analysis must also consider whether—and to what extent—the changes impact PIM practices of the department or organization.

Once the analysis has been performed, the PIM team or executive in charge must consider whether the changes in practices require alterations to privacy policies and procedures. If so, these changes must be made immediately and, if they impact the commitments made in your publicly facing privacy policy, communicated to customers and consumers whose PII your organization maintains. This notice must include the opportunity for the individual to opt-out of the planned use of his or her PII. Individuals who do not opt-out will be subject to the new practices. Although failure to provide such notification has been viewed by the FTC as a violation of Section 5 of the FTC Act, the requirement is now specifically required by the California Online Privacy Protection Act. Again, compliance with this law is required for any online company that collects PII on California residents, regardless of the state in which the company is located.

Another example of careless changes to PIM practices in an online environment comes from 2001 and involves an online retailer. During bankruptcy proceedings, the retailer listed its database of information on 250,000 customers as an asset that could be sold. This ran contra to the retailer's privacy policy, which read in part that:

> Personal information, voluntarily submitted by visitors to our site, such as name, address, billing information and shopping preferences, is never shared with a third party. . . . When you register with [our website], you can rest assured that your information will never be shared with a third party.[93]

The FTC alleged that the company violated Section 5 of the FTC Act by misrepresenting to consumers that personal information would never be shared with third parties and then disclosing, selling, or offering that information for sale in violation of the company's own privacy statement.

Managing Violations and Enforcing Policy

16

Despite your best efforts and the implementation of a comprehensive PIM program, there will always remain a risk of privacy violations by your employees. There are a variety of reasons for employee violations of information management programs. These include:

- **Lack of awareness**—Employees are simply unaware of the requirements of the PIM program due to poor communication and inadequate instruction about the policies and procedures.

- **Confusion**—Employees may become confused about what is required of them under the PIM program. This may arise from changes in organizational structure, changes in job roles and responsibilities, lack of training, and other factors.

- **Inconsistent enforcement and lack of oversight**—Employees who see that policies are not consistently enforced are likely to fall under the impression that they need not comply with those policies.

- **Willful acts**—As we have seen with the theft of PII from one of the nation's largest ISPs, there are employees who will deliberately violate privacy policies and procedures in order to profit through criminal activity.

As mentioned previously, an integral element of the total PIM program should be a requirement that all employees review privacy standards and sign off on their understanding and commitment to abide by them. This effectively eliminates the potential for an employee to claim lack of awareness. It also establishes the consequences of privacy violations, reducing the risk of lawsuits upon employee termination.

Some organizations have implemented strong policies that require employees to report any privacy violations of which they have become aware. For example, the following is from the privacy policy of a major U.S. university:

A. If any university employee or student or teaching assistant or research assistant or other appointee, or any contractor or consultant or vendor to, or business partner to, the university discovers evidence of any apparent violations of this policy they must notify the Privacy Officer immediately and take care to preserve the evidence of violation. Failure to do so is grounds for disciplinary measures up to and including termination of employment or expulsion and other legal actions.

B. The University should actively create a climate which encourages all members of the broad university community (including, but not limited to, patients, research subjects, vendors, external auditors, volunteers, students, research assistants, teaching assistants, faculty, staff, and all other employees, or third parties external to the university), partner institutions and the general public to report to the Privacy Officer instances of credible evidence of possible violations of privacy and security policy.

C. If anyone (including patients, research subjects, vendors, external auditors, volunteers, students, partner institutions, or other third parties external to the university) discovers apparent evidence of any incidental violation of this policy, they should report it to the University Privacy Officer and the University will take appropriate actions to resolve the issue.

These "whistleblower" provisions add another layer of protection in your PIM program by requiring employees who are aware of violations to report them.

Make Sure Employees Understand the Consequences

It is imperative that all employees clearly understand the consequences of violating the PIM program. In addition to being presented with, and required to sign, the policy indicating that they understand consequences of policy violations, employees should be informed that PIM policies are subject to revision and updating as necessary and/or at the discretion of management. If the enterprise-wide privacy acknowledgement indicates that employees must sign, similar statements should be contained in each departmental policy. The departmental privacy policies will obviously differ based on the type of information handled, but a statement outlining the consequence of non-compliance should be included. They should become a standard part of the corporate culture of which every employee is keenly aware.[94]

Sample "Consequences" Policy Statement

> *VIOLATION OF ANY ASPECT OF THIS POLICY MAY RESULT IN DISCIPLINARY ACTION, UP TO AND INCLUDING TERMINATION. Further, theft or assisting another in theft of any Company property, including consumers' personally identifiable information maintained by the Company, is a crime for which you may be criminally prosecuted. As such, you must read and follow this Policy, and seek clarification from your supervisor if you are unclear on any requirement. In addition, be aware that this Policy provides MINIMUM STANDARDS. Your department may provide additional and/or different directives that are required to ensure compliance with specific laws, regulations, and industry requirements.[95]*

Sample Employee "Certification" Statement

> *Signing this document will certify that I have read and understand the Personal Information Management Manual. I also understand that our Company is committed to protecting the personally identifiable information (PII) it collects and maintains and fully complying with all applicable laws and regulations. I will comply with any requirements to preserve the company's PII pursuant to any audit, investigation, or litigation.*
>
> *I understand that violation of any aspect of this policy may result in disciplinary action, up to and including termination. I understand that when I have a concern about a possible violation of this Policy, I have a duty to report the concern to my supervisor. I further understand that this Policy may be modified from time to time by the company.[96]*

Employees should periodically be reminded of the real-world consequences of privacy violations. Examples of problems should be disseminated, and they should clearly convey the aftermath of violations and their impact on the company. This includes informing employees of PIM violations within the organization that have led to terminations and other disciplinary actions, including demotions or the removal of an individual's authorization to access PII. A large ISP that suffered the theft of 92 million email addresses by an employee provides an excellent example of such a communication. In this instance, an internal memo was circulated which clearly stated the impact and repercussions of the theft. The memo read in part:

> *It is a very disturbing fact of life that an employee with criminal intentions can betray our members' trust by working around systems and procedures that are in place to protect data from disclosure. By pursuing this employee, and working so hard to assist law enforcement, we are letting it be known that we will pursue every lead to shut down spammers' abilities to send junk mail to our members. . . . But this case, and our role in its investigation, should also send a clear message: We will absolutely not tolerate wrongdoing by employees. We will do everything we can to uncover abuse and assist law enforcement in prosecuting it. Instances of unethical or illegal behavior threaten our most precious commodity— our members' trust. As a company, we must expect that everyone abide by the highest ethical standards. To accept anything less would be a disservice to the members whom we ultimately serve.[97]*

In the case referenced above, a decision was made not to identify the employee by name. When using an instance of a former employee who was terminated or disciplined for privacy violations, the following rules should be observed:

- Do not use the disciplined employee's name, unless there is a compelling reason to do so, and only with approval from HR and Legal.

- Clearly describe the violation that occurred, and if applicable, why it took place and the consequences to the employee.

- Refer to and/or quote the sections of the policies and/or laws that were violated.

- Describe the real or potential harm caused to the company by the violations.

- Describe what employees can do to avoid committing similar violations.

- Remind employees of the importance of the PIM program as a whole.[98]

There is ample opportunity to provide illustrations of violations and their impact within and outside your organization. These should include examples of consumer complaints and how these can lead to or have led to lawsuits, FTC investigations, and criminal actions by state attorneys general. Again, emphasize the resulting negative publicity from the press and consumer advocacy groups, along with any loss of shareholder value.

The Importance of Consistent PIM Enforcement

In addition to ensuring that the right message about PIM enforcement is delivered to your employees, it is equally important that actual enforcement is done on a consistent basis.

Consistency of enforcement tells employees that your organization is committed to the PIM program, and that they are expected to be equally as committed. It delivers certainty to employees about the consequences of what will occur if policies are violated. This, in turn, can diminish the likelihood of other PIM violations. Further, in an environment of consistent enforcement, employees will not be able to successfully assert that the written policies differed materially from the enforcement of those policies.

Consistency also makes enforcement much easier for supervisors, managers, and the legal department because it demonstrates that the organization does what it says it will do to ensure that employees act in accord with the PIM program. Importantly, consistent enforcement delivers a message of fairness. This means that all violators are subject to the same consequences and will be treated without favoritism or discrimination—an important factor in eliminating post-termination employee lawsuits. In light of the steady flow of such lawsuits, it is critical that no individuals within the organization receive special treatment with regard to PIM violations. While PIM implementation and business unit rules may differ slightly from department to department, each of these rules must be enforced consistently within that department and remain in accord with the organization's overarching policies.

Application of PIM standards also must be consistent with regard to employees who use technology such as laptops or handheld devices, particularly if these are left in the care of employees. Specific policies must be in place and efforts taken within the organization to limit the transfer of PII to these devices. As with all other PIM policies, these must be closely monitored and consistently enforced. This is particularly important with personally owned devices, as these often are not equipped with the data protection technologies employed on your organization's equipment.

Consistency is also critical in communicating your commitment to responsible privacy practices to the outside world. It demonstrates to the FTC, courts, auditors, and shareholders that your organization is serious about personal information management. It also delivers a message to the public and increases their level of comfort in conducting business with your organization. Of course, inconsistent enforcement of your PIM program will inevitably send the wrong message. Lax privacy enforcement carries with it the potential of legal consequences, lost business, and public anger.

Breach Management

If a security breach occurs at your organization, the ultimate cost could be determined by the organization's response. If you react swiftly, fix the problem, and notify the interested parties, the damage may be minimized. Delay, indecision, and attempts to deny or hide the problem, on the other hand, could be disastrous.

There is no such thing as planning in a crisis. During a crisis, people react. The best way to prevent poor crisis management is to be prepared ahead of time. To effectively handle a breach, your organization needs to have two assets in place before the breach occurs: a response team and a breach management plan.

The Response Team

The response team may, and probably should, include many of the same members as your PIM team. As was the case in developing your PIM policies, your team will need representatives from the major areas likely to be involved in any breach response:

- CEO, Chief Privacy Officer, or other executive-level representative
- Legal
- HR
- IT
- Department heads who work with PII
- Customer Service
- Public Relations

When selecting members of the breach response team, you need people who can plan ahead for contingencies and think calmly and rationally. Remember, the purpose of the team is to plan for crises ahead of time. Although members of the team should be able to think on their feet and respond quickly under pressure, it is equally important that they be able to anticipate the unexpected and draft comprehensive solutions.

The Breach Management Plan

The details of your plan will depend upon the nature of your business and the PII you use. As you begin to plan, look at how other companies in your organization's industry have reacted to crises. What type of problems were they most likely to encounter? When those problems occurred, how did they respond? Was it effective?

As the team formulates the breach management plan, it should include:

- **A clear delegation of responsibility**—One person, most likely the executive, should be in charge of making final decisions and organizing the team during a crisis. Another member, perhaps a PR representative, should assume responsibility for all media inquiries and public statements. IT will be in charge of securing the networks and analyzing the extent of the damage. Long before a breach occurs, the roles of each team member in responding to the breach should be clear and documented.

- **Know who must be notified outside of the company**—Depending on the nature of the breach, your first call may need to be to law enforcement. Your team can identify the local police and FBI offices likely to assist them. You should generate lists of consumers or customers who may need to be notified. Some regulators may need formal notification, as well. Find out in advance, so you don't waste previous time deciding these questions after the breach.

- **Resources, internal and external, that may be useful**—Know your organization's limitations. Think of some problems that would be beyond your technical expertise (and if you can't, you're probably not trying hard enough), then identify and select outside help that could be retained if necessary. Although you may think of this as a technological issue, there are a number of professionals who can offer assistance in marketing and public relations, customer assurance, even employee assistance.

- **Have sample responses ready to go**—Obviously, one of the crises your team should be prepared for is PII falling into the wrong hands. Draft sample letters that you would send to customers, clients, and employees, describing the problem, the source, and the organization's response. Do the same for media statements. With prepared samples, it is much easier to simply plug in the specifics instead of drafting a written response on the fly.

- **Plan for communication**—Everybody on the team should know what to do if a breach occurs. Decide the order in which team members will be notified, how they will meet and conference, and how the team's response will be implemented. All team members should have each other's email addresses, emergency telephone numbers, and other vital contact information.

With Lemons, Make Lemonade

When problems present themselves, quick decisions or reactive fixes can have devastating consequences. Any problem involving the misuse of personal information belonging to a customer, client, or employee is likely to be accompanied by fear, if not panic, on the part of the organization. The emotional reaction may be compounded by the uncertainty of financial repercussions that could drag on for years. If you plan now for PIM failures, you will respond better when they occur.

A proper and thoughtful response can have a hugely positive impact for an organization that has made a mistake. Recently, a technology company learned that their human resources contractor suffered a break-in. Laptops containing employee information were taken. In addition to allaying employees' concerns that the information was properly protected, the company immediately purchased ID theft insurance for all employees and commenced a credit monitoring program for all employees as well.

A related point worth making is that technology can alleviate a PII management crisis. In response to identity theft and credit card scams, a European bank provided almost real time notification to customers of purchases made with their credit cards. Similarly, when an FBI email system was breached, the FBI shut down the system and notified users on alternate email addresses about the problem.

Problems will always materialize. By planning your response to the next PII management crisis, you may find the problem will be solved with relative ease.

- **Identify likely short-term and long-term solutions**—As you anticipate the possible breaches that may occur, consider the immediate steps you could take to reassure the public, the government, or your employees. If it is a small breach, the company could offer to purchase identity theft insurance or assist in requesting credit reports. Initial notices could be sent in real time, by IM, or email, so consumers get information from you as soon as possible. A new portion of your website could keep the public and the media up to speed and reinforce your command of the situation.

- **Investigating the problem**—A comprehensive review of your organization's policies, the cause of the breach, and the necessary solutions will be necessary. Your team can identify the best people, inside and outside the organization, to draw on for the investigation. These people should have access to information throughout the breach management process.

Improving Your PIM Program

17

As you know by now, privacy is a business function that does not remain static for long. A good PIM program must be continually updated and improved. Your PIM practices will need to be monitored for their efficacy and legal compliance once up and running. Your PIM oversight team or officer must act as soon as possible to address any problems or weaknesses in the PIM program.

Managing Privacy in a Perpetually Evolving Environment

Your PIM program must be flexible enough to adapt to changes in the way your organization conducts business, as well as changes in the laws and regulations that drive your PIM practices. At the time of this writing, the House and Senate were considering numerous privacy laws addressing wireless telephone directories, list brokers, spyware, offshore transfers of data, and much more. At the same time, several hundred privacy bills were making their way through state legislatures that targeted an even broader array of privacy issues. Privacy law is being interpreted by state and federal courts in every state in the country, including complex and emotionally charged matters such as the USA PATRIOT Act. International privacy laws also continue to evolve rapidly. With all of these changes taking place, the privacy aware organization and its key employees watch for changes that will affect their business. While nearly all laws allow time for organizations to comply with new requirements, legislative monitoring has become a business necessity.

Even minor changes in business practices might require an updating of privacy policies and/or practices. Take for example, a company that decides that, in addition to the basic information it collects on customers (shipping information and credit card number), it would also like a bit of demographic information, including date of birth. Although this company's website does not target children, collecting date of birth from anyone under the age of 13 falls within the COPPA regulations and the company would need to make a number of changes to current practices to fully comply. Or, suppose a company has been filling its own orders, but has grown larger and now wishes to hire a third party to handle this function. Naturally, the new vendor must have customers' shipping information. In each of these examples, the privacy practices and/or the publicly facing privacy policy must change. In instances where the new practice differs materially from the organization's former procedures, it is often necessary to contact consumers whose PII you already maintain and get their consent to the new PIM practices. This is particularly true when an organization makes a decision that it will begin selling customers' PII. If this is contrary to the existing privacy policy, consent must be obtained, as we have seen in a number of FTC actions and settlement agreements. Likewise, if a company's assets change hands (whether through merger, acquisition, bankruptcy, or other transaction), the PII in possession of that company must be maintained in accord with existing privacy policies, or consumer consent must be obtained to handle it in any other manner.

The Murky World of Privacy

In the wake of 9/11, a number of new security laws and legislative initiatives emerged. Many of these laws have been on a collision course with established privacy law. The battle between these interests will likely be fought in court for years to come.

For example, one part of the USA PATRIOT Act requires libraries to disclose certain information to law enforcement. This has been a source of animosity between the government, law enforcement organizations, and library associations. Similarly, in Europe, legislative efforts following the terrorist attacks in Madrid, Spain included efforts to require that ISPs retain email traffic information for up to three years. Opponents quickly criticized the measure as inconsistent with the European Convention on Human Rights.

Because the resolution of these apparent conflicts likely will take some time, a privacy-aware organization must continually check the status of the law and recent court decisions to ensure its PIM practices are consistent with the controlling legal authority in its jurisdiction.

Continuous program improvement should also contain a component by which best practices are monitored on a regular basis. Best practices obviously vary by industry, and it is important to stay apprised of what is working and what is not. For example, financial services and healthcare/pharmaceuticals are highly regulated industries that handle large amounts of PII. Some of the companies in these industries, however, will distinguish themselves with superior PIM strategies. Your organization should always make efforts to stay abreast of how other businesses are succeeding in PIM and learn from the best practices of others.

Periodic Audits

In addition to continuous monitoring, periodic (perhaps annual) audits are an integral component of a successful PIM program. Unlike the continuous monitoring that should be active at all times during the lifespan of the PIM program, audits take a holistic view of the program and ensure that it is compliant with current laws, industry best practices, and business needs. Periodic audits also create a paper trail of compliance with privacy laws and regulations, a fact that is of critical importance from a risk management point of view.

The importance of audits becomes clear when you look at the issue in the context of HIPAA and other federal laws. With HIPAA, for example, the Privacy Rule requires that an organization maintaining electronic protected health information (EPHI) be able to provide to an individual the names of any third parties with whom his or her information was shared. Auditing becomes crucial in ensuring that proper records of data transfers are maintained and that this standard is met. Further, the HIPAA Security Rule requires an internal audit process to determine the identity of individuals in the organization who have access to specific confidential information. The Rule allows for auditing controls that include hardware, software, and/or administrative systems that record the activity on systems containing EPHI. While the Privacy Rule requires accounting for external disclosures of EPHI, the Security Rule requires audit trails. Because HIPAA demands accountability for data use at multiple levels within your organization, periodic and ongoing audits have become a necessity for all covered entities.

The European Union Data Protection Directive and the U.S. Department of Commerce's safe harbor program also require ongoing auditing. This comes in the form of annual "self-certification" that an organization's privacy practices conform to the requirements of the safe harbor framework. The enforcement provisions of the Safe Harbor Rule call for "procedures for verifying that the commitments companies make to adhere to the safe harbor principles have been implemented."[100] The Department of Commerce provides that an organization may verify such attestations and assertions in one of two ways: self-assessment or outside compliance reviews.[101] In the case of third-party audits, the Department of Commerce provides that:

> *Where the organization has chosen outside compliance review, such a review needs to demonstrate that its privacy policy regarding personal information received from the EU conforms to the Safe Harbor Principles, that it is being complied with and that individuals are informed of the mechanisms through which they may pursue complaints. The methods of review may include without limitation auditing, random reviews, use of "decoys," or use of technology tools as appropriate.*[102]

So clearly, in planning the audit, consideration must be given to whether the audit will be conducted internally—by the PIM team, for example—or by a third-party auditor. Careful attention should be paid to any laws that govern this decision, particularly where the PII involved is sensitive in nature. The organization should also consider any industry standard practices regarding third party or internal audits. The decision-making process must include a close look at just how formal and involved the auditing process will be. A third party auditor will likely be more readily prepared to undertake a formal, in-depth audit than the PIM team or other internal resources. Other considerations might include the size and number of locations of the organization and its data; the complexity of the technology used to store, access, and protect PII; and of course, the regulatory environment in which the organization operates. Finally, the maturity of the PIM program must be considered. If this is the first audit after full implementation of the PIM program, a third party audit may provide an unbiased measurement of the new PIM program. For more mature programs, an internal audit may be appropriate.

Upon completion of the audit, positive results should be leveraged to benefit the organization. Specifically, positive outcomes should be publicized. As we keep emphasizing, PIM is not solely about risk management. It is equally important in raising consumers' level of trust in conducting business with you. By publicizing the results, your organization can show its shareholders that solid privacy practices benefit the organization in many ways.

Correcting Failures in the PIM Program

In the event that failures, flaws, or risks to PII are found in your auditing or continuous improvement efforts, steps must be taken to rectify these shortcomings immediately. Of course, the first step in the process is to find and correct the cause of the failure. If the failure is technical in nature, a technical solution is appropriate. It is worth noting that as technology continues to develop at a rapid pace, existing technologies become obsolete with alarming speed. Similarly, external threats to networks and PII are evolving nearly as rapidly as the technology designed to safeguard them. In this environment, it is essential that executives and IT professionals remain consistently apprised of the state of the art in privacy and security systems.

In the case of failures on the part of employees, subsequent steps become a bit more complex. The first step in such instances is simple—correct the problem. This might be as simple as assigning the employee to a position in which he or she no longer handles PII, or simply retraining the employee. Of course, much depends on the seriousness of the violation. If retraining is deemed appropriate, management should consider whether other similarly situated employees should receive the training as well.

In some instances, disciplinary actions may be required. Employees subject to discipline for breach of privacy policy or procedure must first be reminded of the commitment they made to privacy at the commencement of their employment. In cases warranting re-assignment or termination (as determined by HR and legal), care must be taken to ensure that the employee is treated in line with the violation and consistent with the organization's past practices. This is critical to minimize the possibility of post-termination lawsuits.

Failures in the PIM program should be communicated internally, in an appropriate manner, to managers involved in PII, and, in some cases, to all employees who work with PII. If the violation is going to be revealed to a large number of people, care must be taken in deciding whether to identify the party in question. While there is value in setting an example, it must be balanced against the negative impact on employee morale. Do not, however, underestimate the value of communicating about failures. One failure in your PII program is a strong indicator that others may exist. Don't just assume that the failure is the result of the negligence of one individual. It may be the result of policies that are not sufficiently clear to employees. Perhaps the employees have not been trained properly or effectively. These possibilities should be thoroughly investigated through ongoing employee monitoring, employee interviews, and reviews of policies and procedures in question. This interaction provides a wealth of information that can be used to improve the PIM program and reduce, if not eliminate, the possibility of similar mistakes in the future.

In some instances, it will be necessary to communicate failures in the PIM program to consumers. This is particularly true in the instance of data breaches by unauthorized third parties (see discussion of the California SB 1386, in Chapter 6).

Conclusion: The Privacy Aware Business in the 21st Century

You are now armed with a wide-ranging knowledge of the foundational elements of privacy, along with the practical tools you'll need to develop and implement a comprehensive PIM program. That program, if carefully planned and competently operated, will serve the dual purposes of risk management and benefiting the bottom line.

As you go forward operating within the PIM structure, the most important rule to keep in mind is that your PIM program may evolve as the privacy landscape evolves. Privacy law continues to evolve at a rapid pace, not only in the halls of Congress and state legislatures, but also as a result of precedent-setting court decisions and government agency rulings that are occurring by the week. Add up all of the privacy issues that will emerge as technology advances and new media and communications channels are developed, and privacy will only become more daunting for businesses and individuals alike. For all of these reasons, privacy will continue as a crucial business issue. It demands the attention of responsible executives who can keep one eye on the present, and one eye focused sharply on the future. In the end, managing privacy like any information management activity is a process not a project, so be vigilant.

Endnotes

[1] Source: Ponemon Institute.

[2] *See* Shield, Mike, "Spitzer Sues Spyware Firm," *Mediaweek*, April 29, 2005. Available at: http://www.mediaweek.com/mw/news/interactive/article_display.jsp?vnu_content_id=1000903165

[3] Source: Network Solutions, Privacy Survey, February, 2004.

[4] See the Federal Trade Commission Spam Workshop. Available online at: http://www.ftc.gov/bcp/workshops/spam/index.html

[5] "CVS Halts Access Over Web to Data of Loyalty Cards," The *Wall Street Journal*, June 22, 2005.

[6] 2004 Yankelovich State of Consumer Trust—Rebuilding the Bonds of Trust.

[7] Available at: http://www.ftc.gov/opa/2004/04/towerrecords.htm

[8] Available at: http://www.ftc.gov/opa/2003/06/guess.htm

[9] Available at: http://www.ftc.gov/opa/2002/01/elililly.htm

[10] Available at: http://www.ftc.gov/opa/2002/08/microsoft.htm

[11] Chabrow, Eric. "With a D+ on Their Report Card, Federal Security Officers Try a Study Group," *Information Week*, Feb. 16, 2005. Report available at: http://www.gao.gov/new.items/d05262.pdf

[12] Information Security: Internal Revenue Service Needs to Remedy Serious Weaknesses over Taxpayer and Bank Secrecy Act Data. GAO-05-482, April 15. Available at http://www.gao.gov/cgi-bin/getrpt?GAO-05-482. Information Security: Department of Homeland Security Faces Challenges in Fulfilling Statutory Requirements, by Gregory C. Wilshusen, director, information security, before the Subcommittee on Management, Integration, and Oversight, House Committee on Homeland

Security. GAO-05-567T, April 14. Available at: http://www.gao.gov/cgi-bin/getrpt?GAO-05-567T

[13] Samuel Warren and Louis Brandeis, "The Right to Privacy," *Harvard Law Review*, v. 4, no. 5, 193-220 (1890). [Quote is attributable to a contemporary of Brandeis and Warren, a judge Thomas Cooley (see p. 2 of reference).]

[14] Griswold v. Connecticut 381 U.S. 479 (1965).

[15] 28 CFR § 22.2(e).

[16] The EU Directive, for example, requires creation of government data protection agencies, registration of data bases with those agencies, and in some instances prior approval before personal data processing may begin.

[17] "Privacy Chief Takes Aim at Spammers With E-Mail Ruling," *Ottawa Business Journal,* Feb. 21, 2005.

[18] See letter from FTC Commissioner. Available at: http://www.house.gov/markey/Issues/iss_privacy_rep040507.pdf

[19] Strom, Stephanie, "A.C.L.U.'s Search for Data on Donors Stirs Privacy Fears," *New York Times,* December 18, 2004.

[20] FDIC Guidance on Instant Messaging. Cited at http://www.fdic.gov/news/news/financial/2004/fil8404a.html

[21] Red-M Communications Survey.

[22] 16 CFR, Part 603, FACT Act (amends the FCRA).

[23] http://www.consumer.gov/sentinel/ [Multiple citations on fraud and ID theft, chart and graph.]

[24] Saranow, Jennifer, and Ron Lieber, "Freezing Out Identity Theft: Potent State Laws Let Consumers Bar Inquiries Into Their Credit Reports, but There Are Hassles," The *Wall Street Journal,* March 15, 2005, D1.

[25] "Social Security Numbers: Governments Could Do More to Reduce Display in Public Records and on Identity Cards," GAO, November 2004, (GAO-05-59).

[26] *See* Huggins v. Citibank NA, 355 S.C. 329, 585 S.E.2d 225 (S.C. 2003); Polzer v. TRW, Inc. 256 A.D.2d 248 (N.Y. App. Div. 1998). See also Towle, Identity Theft: Myths, Methods and New Law, *Rutgers Computer & Technology Law Journal,* v. 30, pp. 237-326 (2004).

[27] "Retail Ventures Says DSW Shoe Customer Data Stolen," Reuters, March 8, 2005. Available at: http://www.reuters.com/newsArticle.jhtml?storyID=7843601

[28] Morrison, Joanne, "Bank Loses Credit-Card Info of 1.2 Million Federal Workers," Reuters, February 26, 2005.

[29] Sayvas, Antony, "Biggest ever data theft culprit faces long sentence," Computer Weekly.com, August 15, 2005.

[30] The Associated Press, "ChoicePoint Execs Sold Shares After Breach," February 25, 2005. The Associated Press, "SEC Probing ChoicePoint Stock Sales," March 4, 2005.

[31] "Identity Theft: What's in a name," *The Economist,* March 5, 2005.

[32] Gutner, Toddi, "What's Lurking in Your PC? How to keep spyware from tracking your habits—or highjacking your computer," Business Week, Oct. 4, 2004, 108-110.

[33] Based on September 2004 survey conducted by the Ponemon Institute and sponsored by TRUST-e.

[34] 2004 Yankelovich State of Consumer Trust—Rebuilding the Bonds of Trust.

[35] Ibid.

[36] Press Release, "Senator Feinstein Asks Credit Card Companies to Describe Steps to Notify Individuals, Protect them from Identity Theft in Wake of Massive Data Breach," June 21, 2005. Available at: http://feinstein.senate.gov/05releases/r-databreach.htm

[37] 45 CFR §§ 164.502(b), 164.514(d).

[38] 15 USC, Subchapter I, Sec. 6801-6809, GLBA.

[39] 15 U.S.C. § 1681 et seq, FCRA.

[40] 16 CFR Part 602, FACT Act.

[41] 45 CFR §§ 164.502(b), 164.514(d).

[42] 16 CFR 316, CAN-SPAM.

[43] 16 CFR Part 312, the Children's Online Privacy Protection Act.

[44] 5 U.S.C. § 552a(b).

[45] Hasson, Judi, "VA toughens security after PC disposal blunders," 26 August, 2002. Available at: http://www.fcw.com/fcw/articles/2002/0826/news-va-08-26-02.asp

[46] Magid, Larry, "Hard drives dumped; information isn't." Available at: http://www.whitecanyon.com/presscenter/article_mn_01_03.php

[47] Garfinkel, Simson, "Hard-Disk Risk: Are all those old hard drives you're getting rid of free of important company data? Don't be so sure," *CSO* magazine, April 2003. Available at: http://www.simson.net/clips/2003/2003.CSO.04.Hard_disk_risk.htm

[48] The Online Privacy Protection Act of 2003, Cal. Bus. & Prof. Code, 22575–22579 (2004).

[49] Thibodeau, Patrick, "New Vermont 'opt-in' privacy law faces legal challenge," *Computerworld*, February 7, 2002.

[50] Specht v. Netscape Communications Corp., 306 F.3d 17 (2d Cir. 2002).

[51] 18 U.S.C. § 2701(a)(1), 2707(a), SCA (part of ECPA).

[52] Pub. L. No. 108-187, 117 Stat. 2699.

[53] Federal Trade Commission, "The CAN-SPAM Act: Requirements for Commercial Emailers." Available at: http://www.ftc.gov/bcp/conline/pubs/buspubs/canspam.htm

[54] Federal Trade Commission, "The CAN-SPAM Act: Requirements for Commercial Emailers." Available at: http://www.ftc.gov/bcp/conline/pubs/buspubs/canspam.htm

[55] CAN-SPAM, Sec 7 (f)3.

56 California Civil Code §1798.29 and 1798.82–1798.84.

57 47 U.S.C. § 551.

58 20 U.S.C. § 1232G; 34 CFR Part 99.

59 Available at: http://thomas.loc.gov/cgi-bin/bdquery/z?d109: h.r.00418:

60 "The Real ID Act Raises Privacy Issues," Morning Edition, National Public Radio, May 6, 2005. Available at: http://www.npr. org/templates/story/story.php?storyId=4632952&sourceCode=RSS

61 15 U.S.C. § 1681. [Definition of "credit report"/"consumer report" in the document.]

62 12 U.S.C. §§ 3401–3422.

63 12 U.S.C. 1829b, 12 U.S.C. 1951 et seq, and 31 U.S.C. 5311 et seq.

64 45 CFR 164.501, 164.508(a)(3).

65 45 CFR Parts 160, 162, 164.

66 Landro, Laura, "The Doctor is Online: Secure Messaging Boosts the Use of Web Consultations," The *Wall Street Journal*, Sep. 2, 2004, D1.

67 Ibid.

68 Randolph A. Kahn, Esq., and Barclay T. Blair, *Information Nation: Seven Keys to Information Management Compliance*, AIIM, 2004.

69 Ibid.

70 Lemos, Robert, "Payroll site closes on security worries," CNET News.com, February 23, 2005.

71 *See* Electronic Communications Privacy Act, 18 USC 2510, et seq.

72 Watkins v. L.M. Berry & Co., 704 F.2d 577, 583 (11th Cir. 1983).

73 *See* United States v. Slanina, No. 00-20926 (5th Cir. 2002).

[74] *See* United States v. Angevine, No. 01-6097 (10th Cir. 2001).

[75] *Americans and Online Privacy: The System is Broken,* 2004, Annenberg Public Privacy Center, University of PA.

[76] http://www.insight-mag.com/insight/04/11-12/col-3-pt-1-CurrentAffairs.asp

[77] Mark Maremont, "New Privacy Leak: Some Mutual Funds Reveal Clients' Data," The *Wall Street Journal*, March 23, 2005.

[78] "Efficient Confidentiality for Privacy, Security, and Confidential Business Information," by Peter P. Swire, Brookings-Wharton Papers on Financial Services, (Brookings, 2003).

[79] Randolph A. Kahn, Esq., and Barclay T. Blair, *Information Nation: Seven Keys to Information Management Compliance,* AIIM, 2004.

[80] The Online Privacy Protection Act of 2003, Cal. Bus. & Prof. Code, 22575–22579 (2004).

[81] Li Yuan, "Companies Face System Attacks From Inside, Too," The *Wall Street Journal*, June 1, 2005.

[82] Privacy Policy Sample cited from: http://www.bbbonline.org/privacy/sample_privacy.asp

[83] Winstein, Keith J., "Bluetooth Gear May Be Open To Snooping," The *Wall Street Journal*, June 16, 2005.

[84] The Commission's final decision and order against Microsoft is available at: http://www.ftc.gov/os/2002/12/microsoftdecision.pdf. The complaint is available at: http://www.ftc.gov/os/2002/12/microsoftcomplaint.pdf

[85] 45 CFR Section 164.504(e)(2)(ii).

[86] Jessica Davis, "Processors Get Hardened," *Electronic Business,* Dec. 1, 2004.

[87] Bergman, Hannah, "FDIC Offers, Solicits Ideas on Stopping ID Theft," *American Banker* Vol. 169, Issue 240, December 16, 2004.

[88] Pulliam, Daniel, "Identity theft of FDIC employees leads to bank fraud, union says," GovExec.com Daily Briefing, June 17, 2005.

[89] *American Banker,* June 17, 2005.

[90] 15 U.S.C. §§ 41–58.

[91] 15 U.S.C. §§ 41–58.

[92] "Tower Record Settles FTC Charges," Press Release, Federal Trade Commission, April 21, 2004. Available at: http://www.ftc.gov/opa/2004/04/towerrecords.htm

[93] FTC v. Toysmart.com, LLC and Toysmart.com, Inc. Cited at: http://www.ftc.gov/opa/2000/07/toysmart2.htm

[94] Randolph A. Kahn, Esq., and Barclay T. Blair, *Information Nation: Seven Keys to Information Management Compliance,* AIIM, 2004.

[95] Adapted from: Randolph A. Kahn, Esq., and Barclay T. Blair, *Information Nation: Seven Keys to Information Management Compliance,* AIIM, 2004. For informational purposes only. Seek the advice of counsel before adopting any Personal information management policy element.

[96] Ibid.

[97] AOL internal memorandum. Available at: http://www.internalmemos.com/memos/memodetails.php?memo_id=2323

[98] Randolph A. Kahn, Esq., and Barclay T. Blair, *Information Nation: Seven Keys to Information Management Compliance,* AIIM, 2004.

[99] Chris Woodward, "Fliers lose laptops at airport checkpoints," *USA Today,* February 19, 2002.

[100] U.S. Department of Commerce, Safe Harbor Overview. Cited at: http://www.export.gov/safeharbor/sh_overview.html

[101] U.S. Department of Commerce. Cited at http://www.export.gov/safeharbor/Faq7verifFINAL.htm

[102] Ibid.

Index

accountability, 16, 88-89, 111

ACLU *See* American Civil Liberties Union

acquisitions and mergers, 35, 89, 135-136, 148

AMA *See* American Management Association

American Civil Liberties Union, 22

American Management Association, 25

audits, compliance *See* privacy audits

authentication, 8, 28, 38, 111, 119, 122, 131, 132

backup tapes, 12, 32, 75

Bank Secrecy Act, 68

banking *See* financial industry

best practices, 92, 108, 118, 121, 149, 150

Better Business Bureau, xii, 114-116

Bill of Rights, 15

blogs, 30, 97

Bluetooth, 118

Brandeis, Louis, 15

BSA *See* Bank Secrecy Act

Cable Communications Policy Act, 59

California privacy laws, 31, 47 *See also* California Database Protection Act

California Database Protection Act, 34, 58-59, 131, 152

California Health and Human Services Agency, 59

California Online Privacy Protection Act, 50, 108-109, 135

California SB 1386 *See* California Database Protection Act

Canada *See* CAN-SPAM Act; *See* Personal Information Protection and Electronic Documents Act

CAN-SPAM Act, 3, 47, 56-58, 99, 103, 106

cell phones, 29, 30

CEO *See* responsibilities, Chief Executive Officer

change management, 122, 134-135, 147-148

Chief Executive Officer *See* responsibilities, Chief Executive Officer

Chief Privacy Officer *See* privacy officers

children, 47, 94, 113, 115, 147-148

Children's Online Privacy Protection Act, xiii, 3, 47, 103, 104, 113, 148,

ChoicePoint, Inc., 33-34, 35

click-through agreements, 52

compliance monitoring, 131-135

    by third parties, 10-11, 22, 120, 129, 134

response to, 145
warning signs, 24
IIF *See* information in identifiable form
IM *See* instant messaging
information in identifiable form, 16-17
information management compliance, 81
Information Nation: Seven Keys to Information Management
    Compliance, 80, 81
information technology solutions, 125-126, 151
instant messaging, 1, 9, 26-28, 30
Internal Revenue Service (U.S.), 13
international businesses, 19
IRS *See* Internal Revenue Service (U.S.)
key logging software, 123
laptop computers
    security, 126, 142
    theft, xi, 12, 75, 127, 145
law enforcement, 37, 66, 85, 144, 148
lawsuits, 10, 141, 151
license agreements *See* click-through agreements
loyalty cards, 8-9
managers *See* responsibilities, managers
medical records, 30, 38, 69-72, 88, 95, 121-122, 149
Microsoft Corporation, 11
mobile devices, 118 *See also* laptop computers;
    See also cell phones
MTS, Inc., 11
NASD *See* National Association of Securities Dealers
National Association of Securities Dealers, 133
national identification system, 60
New York State Attorney General Office, 22, 36, 129
notice *See* notification
notification
of privacy policies, xi, 7, 16, 17, 22, 38-40, 45, 50-51, 52, 64-65,
    66, 69, 101, 106, 113, 114-116, 135
of security breaches, 43-44, 58-59, 102, 144, 145, 152
opting-in, 5, 52, 106
opting-out, 5, 51-52, 56-57, 63, 64, 106, 135
outsourcing, 20
passwords *See* authentication
penalties, xiii, 7, 21, 22, 36, 57-58, 72, 102, 129
personal computers, recycling, 49
Personal Information Protection and Electronic
    Documents Act, 17, 99

The Enterprise Content Management Association

AIIM Headquarters

1100 Wayne Avenue, Suite 1100
Silver Spring, MD 20910
Phone: 800.477.2446 or 301.587.8202
Fax: 301.587.2711
E-mail: aiim@aiim.org
www.aiim.org

European Office

The IT Centre, 8 Canalside
Lowesmoor Wharf, Worcester
United Kingdom WR1 2RR
Phone: +44 (0) 1905.727.600
Fax: +44 (0) 1905.727.609
www.aiim.org.uk

AIIM is the international authority on Enterprise Content Management (ECM)—the tools and technologies used to capture, manage, store, preserve, and deliver content and documents related to organizational processes. ECM enables four key business drivers: Continuity, Collaboration, Compliance, and Costs.

For over 60 years, AIIM has been the leading non-profit organization focused on helping users to understand the challenges associated with managing documents, content, records, and business processes. Today, AIIM is international in scope, independent, implementation-focused, and, as the representative of the entire ECM industry—including users, suppliers, and the channel—acts as the industry's intermediary.

As a neutral and unbiased source of information, AIIM serves the needs of its members and the industry through the following activities.

MARKET EDUCATION—AIIM provides events and information services that help users specify, select, and deploy ECM solutions to solve organizational problems.

- *AIIM E-DOC Magazine*
  AIIM's bi-monthly print publication with more than 30,000 subscribers in North America. Each issue contains intelligent articles, case studies, thought-provoking columns, and lessons-learned.

- *M-iD Magazine (Managing Information and Documents)*
  The leading publication, read by thousands of document management professionals in the United Kingdom. Each issue focuses on the needs of individuals responsible for the capture, storage and preservation, management, processing, and delivery of information and documents.

- *Wall Posters*
  Thousands of office walls have been plastered with these graphic illustrations on ECM, Records Management, Compliance, and more.

- *AIIM Webinars*
  Provide education on the key issues and trends affecting the industry and typically attract over 500 attendees per session.

- *Online Solution Centers*
  Join hundreds of AIIM web visitors at an AIIM Online Solution Center. Get focused articles, presentations, research studies, and more, for the Financial Services and Healthcare industry, and Federal/State/Local Government.

PROFESSIONAL DEVELOPMENT—AIIM provides an educational roadmap for the industry.

- *ECM & ERM Certificate Program*
  Our ECM & ERM Certificate Programs provide instruction on the Why?,

What?, and How? of Enterprise Content Management and Electronic
Records Management via Web-based and/or classroom courses.

- **AIIM Expo and Conference**
  The leading industry event for Enterprise Content & Document
  Management, which encompasses all the technologies that are used to
  capture, manage, share, and store documents and digital content.

- **ECM Solutions Seminar**
  General and vertically focused educational seminars held in 20 cities
  throughout the U.S. and Canada, help educate professionals with information on the latest industry trends, key business drivers, case study
  examples, solutions, and more.

- **IM Expo**
  The major educational event for the ECM industry, held in five or six
  locations each year across the United Kingdom.

- **Info Ireland**
  A two-day educational event held annually in Dublin, Ireland.

PEER NETWORKING—AIIM creates opportunities that allow
users, suppliers, consultants, and the channel to engage and con-
nect with one another—through chapters, networking groups,
programs, partnerships, and the Web.

- **AIIM Chapters**
  A network of 39 chapters in North America providing educational and
  networking opportunities at the local level for AIIM members.

- **AIIM Partners**
  A global network of organizations similar to AIIM committed to helping
  grow the industry.

INDUSTRY ADVOCACY—AIIM acts as the voice of the ECM
industry in key standards organizations, with the media, and
with government decision-makers.

- **AIIM Standards**
  AIIM is an ANSI (American National Standards Institute) accredited
  standards development organization. AIIM also holds the Secretariat

for the ISO (International Organization for Standardization) committee focused on Information Management Compliance issues, TC171.

- ***Industry Watch***

  Industry research reports provide intelligent information about user trends and perceptions several times a year.

MEMBERSHIP—Through year-round support, AIIM offers several types of membership to suit your needs. Select the one that's best for you, and become a recognized leader in the ECM industry. Increase visibility for your company, develop standards for the industry, get industry information and research, and network with industry professionals and peers.

Professional Membership

(For users of ECM products and services.)

Education, industry research, toolkits, awards, committees, and discounts.

Trade and Advisory Trade Membership

(For suppliers of ECM products and services.)

Comprehensive market exposure and increased visibility for your company, products, and services.

Document Management Service Provider Membership

(For VARs, VADs, systems integrators, and consultants.)

Specialized training and education, company visibility, annual forum, and networking.

Kahn Consulting, Inc.

157 Leonard Wood North

Highland Park, IL 60035

847-266-0722

www.KahnConsultingInc.com

Kahn Consulting, Inc. (KCI) is a consulting firm specializing in the legal, compliance, and policy issues of information technology and information lifecycle management. Through a range of services including information and records management program development; electronic records and email policy development; Information Management Compliance audits; product assessments; legal and compliance research; and education and training, KCI helps its clients address today's critical issues in an ever-changing regulatory and technological environment. Based in Chicago, KCI provides its services to Fortune 500 companies and government agencies in North America and around the world. More information about KCI, its services and its clients can be found online at: www.KahnConsultingInc.com.

where information lives®

EMC Corporation
176 South Street
Hopkinton, MA 01748
508 435 1000
www.emc.com

EMC Corporation. Where information lives.

Who we are

EMC Corporation is the world leader in information infrastructure products, services, and solutions. We are the information storage standard for every major computing platform and are caretakers for more than two-thirds of the world's most essential information. We help enterprises of all sizes manage information as it grows and changes value through information lifecycle management. **Our commitment is to the success of our customers—and our passion is for the life of information.**

What we do

Our mission is to help our customers get the maximum value from their information. We help enterprises of all sizes manage their growing volumes of information—from the time of its creation to its archival and eventual disposal—through information lifecycle management. EMC storage and information management solutions are the foundation of this mission. An EMC information infrastructure unifies networked storage technologies, storage platforms, software, and services to help organizations better and more cost-effectively manage, use, protect, and share their information assets.

Our customers

We serve customers of all sizes. They range from the world's largest banks and financial service firms to local hospitals, manufacturers, retailers, small and medium-size businesses, and consumers. We strive to create the industry's most positive total customer experience through the best technology, solutions, and services. EMC delivers business value by reducing costs, minimizing risks, improving total cost of ownership, helping customers gain competitive advantages, accelerating time-to-solution, and increasing business agility.

Information lifecycle management

Information lifecycle management (ILM) is the ability to cost-effectively and strategically align information infrastructure with business needs based on information's changing value. EMC, the world leader in ILM innovation, assists businesses in extracting the most value from their information—at the lowest possible cost—throughout its lifecycle.

Implementing an information lifecycle management strategy enables enterprises of all sizes to quickly and cost-efficiently address changing service levels, regulatory compliance issues, business continuity needs, growing and changing application demands, shifting market conditions, and emerging opportunities.

Worldwide presence

Established in 1979 and based in Hopkinton, Massachusetts, EMC is represented by more than 100 sales offices and distribution partners in more than 50 countries and has the world's largest storage-dedicated direct sales and service force. EMC has manufacturing plants in Massachusetts, North Carolina, and Ireland and R&D facilities in Massachusetts, North Carolina, India, and Japan with customer support centers in Australia, Massachusetts, Ireland, and Japan.

Many of the world's major computer companies resell EMC's systems and software, including Dell, NEC, Fujitsu Siemens Computers, Unisys, Groupe Bull, and NCR. EMC has also formed alliances with leading software, networking, and services companies, including Cisco, Microsoft, SAP, Oracle, Accenture, and EDS to better serve our mutual customers.

With 2005 revenues of nearly $10 billion, EMC employs 25,000 people worldwide. The company's stock is traded on the New York Stock Exchange under the symbol EMC and is a component of the S&P 500 Index.

To learn more about EMC's products, services, and solutions, visit www.EMC.com or call 1-866-464-7381.

F R S Y T H E

Delivering the business value of IT.[SM]

Forsythe Technology, Inc.
7770 Frontage Rd.
Skokie, IL 60077
http://www.forsythe.com
800-843-4488

Established in 1971, Forsythe is a leading national provider of technology infrastructure solutions, serving organizations across all industries, including many Fortune 1000 companies.

Forsythe acts as a trusted advisor, helping organizations manage the cost and risk of their information technology infrastructure. Forsythe does this by functioning as a single point of contact while providing technology and business consulting services, technology leasing services, and value-added reseller services. Forsythe offers solutions that address the complete technology lifecycle — including assessment, design, validation, planning, integration, management, procurement, and financing.

Forsythe Offerings

IT Advisory Solutions

IT Strategy
• IT Service Management
• IT Infrastructure Strategy, Planning and Program Management

Business Continuity/Disaster Recovery
• Risk Evaluation
• Strategy Review and Development
• Policy Review and Development
• Plan Review and Development
• Risk Mitigation
• Crisis Management

Information Security
• Risk Evaluation
• Strategy Review and Development
• Policy Review and Development

Data Center Services
• Sourcing and Consolidation Strategy
• Data Center Optimization
• Facility Risk Evaluation
• Site Selection and Planning

- Facility Design and Construction Management
- Relocation Strategy
- Relocation Planning
- Relocation Execution

IT Infrastructure Solutions
Infrastructure Management
- IT Optimization
- Enterprise Systems Management

Server Infrastructure
- Server Optimization
- Highly Available Server Architecture
- Virtualization and Partitioning
- Database and Application Optimization
- Server Technology Sourcing

Forsythe has achieved EMC Velocity Signature Partner status through proven best practices, business strategies, and processes in the storage solution arena. This designation also acknowledges Forsythe's nation-wide coverage by storage specialists who have achieved the highest level of EMC-specific training. Forsythe has the experience and documented success assessing information-centric infrastructures, which has earned us recognition as an Authorized Services Network (ASN) member. Forsythe is also an eProven Integrator with expertise deploying the complete Symmetrix and CLARiiON line of products.

EMC Corporation is a leader in information storage systems, software, networks, and services. EMC Automated Networked Storage combines SAN, NAS, and CAS environments into an integrated networked storage infrastructure. It unifies networked storage technologies, storage platforms, software, and services to enable organizations to better and more cost-effectively manage, protect, and share information. As a result, customers are able to reduce costs through consolidation of storage and server resources, centralize and automate manual storage management tasks, and improve overall business continuity and flexibility.

Additional Forsythe certifications — EMC Authorized Services Network (ASN) member

- EMC Technology Architect
- EMC Implementation Engineer
- EMC Storage Administrator

Forsythe functions as a single point of contact through which its customers can manage the cost and risk of their information technology infrastructure. For more information, visit www.forsythe.com or contact us at 800-443-4488.

About the Authors

Randolph A. Kahn, ESQ.

Randolph A. Kahn, ESQ. is an educator and author of dozens of published works including *"Information Nation Warrior,"* *"Information Nation: Seven Keys to Information Management Compliance"* and *"E-Mail Rules."* Mr. Kahn was the recipient of the Britt Literary Award in 2004 for an article entitled "Records Management & Compliance: Making the Connection" and in 2005 for an article entitled "Stand and Deliver." He is an internationally recognized authority on the legal, compliance, and policy issues of information technology and information, and trusted advisor and consultant to Fortune 500 companies, governmental agencies, and court systems.

As founder of Kahn Consulting, Inc., Mr. Kahn leads a team of information management, regulatory, compliance and technology professionals who serve as consultants and advisors to major institutions around the globe. Each year Mr. Kahn speaks around the globe to corporate and government institutions. In addition, Mr. Kahn teaches "Legal Issues in Records and Information Management" at George Washington University.

Daniel J. Goldstein, ESQ.

Daniel J. Goldstein, ESQ. is a privacy consultant in the San Francisco Bay Area and a member of the State Bar of California. Mr. Goldstein specializes in helping businesses comply with the expanding volume of privacy and data protection requirements, with a focus on multinational companies transferring confidential and personally identifiable information across international borders.

Barclay T. Blair

Barclay T. Blair is a consultant and internationally acclaimed speaker and author specializing in the compliance, policy, and management issues of information technology. Mr. Blair advises Global 2000 companies, software and hardware vendors, and government agencies on a broad range of information management compliance issues. Mr. Blair is an executive editor of the American Bar Association's PKI Assessment Guidelines, participated in the development of a protocol for secure, digitally signed documents, and is the author a draft *ISO* standard addressing long-term electronic records preservation.

Mr. Blair has written and edited dozens of publications, speaks internationally on information management compliance matters, and is an instructor at George Washington University. Mr. Blair has edited and contributed to several books, including: *Email Rules* (AMACOM Books: 2003); *Secure Electronic Commerce* (Prentice Hall: 2001); *and Professional XML* (Wrox: 2000). Mr. Blair is the co-author of *Information Nation: Seven Keys to Information Management Compliance* (2004) and *Information Nation Warrior* (2005).

Mr. Blair has presented to industry groups such as the American Counsel of Life Insurers, American Bar Association, BNA Litigation Forum, the World Wide Web Consortium (W3C), ARMA International, AIIM International, Society of Quality Assurance, the PKI Forum, the National Automated Clearinghouse Association and at the Managing Electronic Records conference. Mr. Blair is frequently interviewed by media outlets such as *Wall Street & Technology, Compliance Reporter,* and *US News and World Report.*

Mr. Blair is Director of the IT Compliance Practice at Kahn Consulting and may be contacted at: bblair@KahnConsultingInc.com or 403-638-9302.